LOVE AGAIN

Sharla Hintz

To Makenna, Josiah, Drake and Emery.
You show me the art in living.

ACKNOWLEDGEMENTS

To my children who lived this story with me;

To my family who gave me support, rest, and wisdom as needed;

To Craig and Tricia Cunningham who practically singlehandedly saved our marriage - Tricia, most of the wise things I did were because of you;

To Mike and Shelly Ballard who didn't let something like a horrendous scandal scare them away – Shelly, you are one of the truest people I know;

To the youth leaders and church members who sent cards and money in the mail, prayed for us, and held out an olive branch;

To Steven Baker who challenged me to pursue excellence and then showed me how;

To Ed and Dawn Frederiksen who know us completely and love us anyway – Dawn, you've been my friend as far back as I can remember and that makes me happy;

To my husband who not only gave me something to write about, but had the gumption to make the ending a happy one;

And to the Lord Jesus Christ, my true north;

Thank you.

THE EVENTS OF OCTOBER 30, 2004

My whole life shattered in the space of a blink: the sum of all those seconds my eyes were shut.

I was immersed in the raising of four small children while my husband, Mike, was a respected youth pastor at a large, conservative church in Des Moines, Iowa. I worked alongside my husband, my soul mate, to give our kids a happy childhood and keep up with all that our life demanded. What I didn't understand, didn't have an inkling of, was that my husband wasn't really there beside me.

Just after supper, Mike said we needed to discuss something, and I told him we could talk after the kids were in bed. Although I didn't know what he was going to say, my stomach felt heavy and raw - like I had devoured a large helping of gravel. I tended to my mental to-do list that night, and my arms felt out of sync with my hands. I remember being surprised as too much shampoo filled my cupped palm and spilled over my fingers as I tried to scrub the dirt of life off of my innocent towheads. I also remember my hands trembling as I tediously fastened the final touches on the costumes our kids would wear trick-or-treating the next day. I don't remember what story Mike told the kids that night, but I remember avoiding eye contact with him when he made them laugh. I cried as I said good-night to Makenna, the oldest, and therefore, the last child to go to bed. I remember that clearly.

I reached for the piles of clean laundry, and told Mike he could talk as I folded the clothes. I remember shaping a small sweatshirt into a tidy square. My hands were still shaking.

I was exhausted from one of the worst weeks of my life.

Our seventeen-year-old babysitter had written a letter describing inappropriate sexual episodes between her and Mike. The letter was addressed to her dad, who had died many years earlier, and was found by her mom and step-father. They confronted Mike, but he denied the charge. The accusation shocked me, and I rejected it completely. I believed it was impossible. With fierce loyalty, I stood by Mike's side and defended him. I had worked with teenage girls for thirteen years and knew it was possible for them to develop crushes on coaches, pastors, teachers, and other male role models in their lives. I mistakenly assumed this letter was the result of just such a fleeting crush. She was my go-to babysitter and had become like a little sister to me. I was numb with shock that such a document even existed and wholeheartedly believed Mike could not have participated in such horrifying behavior.

For days I rejected such a terrible possibility…

Mike was uncharacteristically quiet.

However, I sensed a change the moment he returned home from work and walked through the front door like only a man worn out from a lie can walk. As we cared for our kids that evening, ghosts stood in the corners of each room and screamed things I didn't want to know. I sensed the imminent destruction of our marriage, my security, our friendships, and the structure that defined our lives, and I attacked the menial task of laundry attempting to minimize the severity of what Mike was about to say. I can't recall his actual words. That memory has turned into a Charlie Brown scene where the speaker's voice is distorted and incomprehensible. I know that he confessed to stomping all over our marriage vows, belittling our relationship, and abusing our love. Those weren't the words he used.

It's uncanny how parts of traumatic times stand out in your memory in painful clarity, too easily recalled, and other parts blur into a fuzzy vagueness, lost forever.

I watched in stunned silence as he uttered various English words whose round sounds floated through the air and landed like the sharp edge of a knife in my ear. My hands itched alarmingly so I examined them, ignoring the incomprehensible noises Mike was saying at me. I searched my palms and fingers for a rash, but when no red bumps were evident, I scratched one hand with the other over and over until the skin became raw. The scratchy fabric from my socks beset my feet; my legs went completely numb. A deafening roar filled the space between my ears, and sickly tingles raced across my scalp.

The letter was true.

As soon as I heard the facts, my mind rejected them—it was not possible. My head spun as my brain unsuccessfully tried to comprehend the horrible truth I was being told. I clearly remember throwing the clothes I had carefully folded. I have no idea how Mike responded to my laundry-throwing fit. I have only vague memories of him crying quietly as I screamed, but I have a clear picture of him in my mind with socks lying across his head and shoulders and in his lap. I cannot recall anything he might have said, and I don't even know if he felt insulted at my sock assault. I remember wishing that the socks were dirty instead of clean.

No matter how much I wish I could, I will never forget the utter anguish that nearly crushed the life out of me. Agony wrapped around me like a snake and squeezed until breathing was a great chore. I even tore at my neck in an attempt to alleviate the strangling sensation, and, when I found nothing there, I ripped the neck of my T-shirt in a moment of adrenaline-induced strength.

I don't remember anything after that until seven hours later at 3:00 AM. I was lying in bed wide-awake and alone - my body succumbed to exhaustion. I desperately began to pray. I accosted the Lord fervently, relentlessly, and ceaselessly. Even as I fell into moments of sleep, I awoke still beseeching and begging. I was not asking for God's grace; I was not saying the Lord's Prayer. I was not even piously contemplating the great good that God must have in store for me after I passed through this trial. No. I was passionately demanding that my husband would die. Immediately. Before the sun rose. I knew God had the power to do such things, and I implored Him to act swiftly.

I knew I would rather explain to my children that their father had died than tell them he had chosen his own selfishness over us. Then we could all live in the blissful pardon that is bestowed on the dead as they are lowered into the earth.

The difference between happily ever after and torn asunder is sometimes wrought in one day. Hours before the laundry-throwing conversation, the death of my husband would have been tragic and unbearable. The day after his life-altering confession, his death would have been convenient, and I would have considered it the greatest of all blessings.

When the sun finally rose, I picked up a pen and sat on my bed. Convinced that my prayers had worked and I was about to discover the body of my husband, I wanted to write down some of the thoughts flying around inside my head. I stared at the blank page begging the white pureness of it to swallow me and then wrote:

Good-bye, blind trust; you let me down.
Good-bye, happily married; you aren't.
Good-bye, fun times; you are shallow.
Good-bye, caring wife; it is not enough.
Good-bye, team; I guess we aren't.
Good-bye, proud wife; I'm embarrassed.
Good-bye, loving eyes; they've been opened.
Good-bye, hard work; it doesn't matter.
Good-bye, happy memories; you are tainted.
Good-bye, happily ever after; I guess it isn't.
I am going to bury you, and the grave will hold you tight.
You won't be alone—the best part of me will be with you.

Since I had slept in my clothes, I only had to manage to brush my teeth before bracing myself to find my dead husband somewhere in the house. I took a deep breath and walked into the kitchen where he was standing, very alive, at the sink. He told me later that he had also spent the sleepless night praying. He begged God for forgiveness, help, and miracles.

"God should not have let you live through the night," I said, voice quivering.

"I actually completely agree," he whispered.

"I despise you." The sight of him standing in the kitchen infuriated me. I couldn't believe that God had not smote him. He didn't deserve life, and I couldn't face what my future had become. I didn't trust myself to speak, but I had written a note I intended to shove into his pocket when I found his lifeless body. I handed it to him and he read, "I cannot imagine a more horrible reality than this moment. And the moments stretch on with no end in sight. I am trapped in this torture. All these years, I have supported you, had babies, kept the house; I have been giving, but you have been taking. You took my faithfulness for granted and danced in your own lust leaving me to act the part of an idiot. You have spit on my virtue and my honor."

"I know. You're right," he whispered when he finished reading. Even in my anger, his puffy, red eyes pricked my heart, and the prick felt like another betrayal.

"I have lost years of my life to you and the trap called happily ever after. I have lost years of my life just trying to survive the night, but I would gladly die immediately just to take a last breath without feeling like I'm inhaling shards of glass."

"I'm so sorry, Sharla."

"Don't say my name!"

"What should I call you?"

"Sorrow. Or Pain. Maybe Death. That is who I am now."

ABOUT A BOY

I first saw Mike in the summer of 1985, and he mesmerized me. His shaggy hair, the color of sunshine reflected on the top of a very still lake, reminded me of a lion, and his essence seemed too large for the body of a fifteen-year-old boy.

I lived in Des Moines, Iowa, but during my junior high and high school summers I worked as a nanny for my aunt and uncle who ran a youth camp in rural Iowa. I met Mike the summer between eighth and ninth grade. Although he stepped off the same kind of bus as all the other sweaty, gangly kids, he took my breath away. His stunning features reminded me of the boys in the posters I had taped to my bedroom wall.

It was quickly clear to me that Mike lived outside the lines. His mind lacked that annoying and invisible panel of peers we all seem to consult as we constantly wonder what others are thinking of us. He had the spirit of an eagle on the wind in a body with eyes the color of a blue flame. He swam in the forbidden river without a moment's hesitation, as if danger wouldn't think of inconveniencing him. He charmed extra cookies out of the menacing camp cook and handed them out like compliments to the squeaky-voiced boys in his cabin.

On the last day of camp, my two cousins, who I was babysitting, woke up from their nap sweaty and red-cheeked. Danae's hair was a nest of sticky curls, and Donny's T-shirt was pasted to his skin. Sweat was snaking down my back and drenching the waistband of my jean shorts. Summers in Iowa usually felt like a small bathroom after a hot shower. I grabbed their chubby hands and led them to the air-conditioned auditorium on the way to the snack shack to buy some cold Cokes. I heard some disjointed music emanating from the stage, but I opened the auditorium door and walked in anyway. I spotted the door on the opposite side of the room, my intended exit, but then I froze.

A thin boy with greasy hair plunked out a tune on the keyboard and a red-haired boy with a face full of pimples attempted a semi steady drumbeat while Mike sang into the microphone. I don't recall the words of the song. I know the boys with Mike laughed at the humor of it, but I thought I would melt at the sound of that voice.

In a place full of teenage egos and insecurities, the scene on the stage seemed as unlikely as the prom queen attending a sleepover with the top scorers of the spelling bee.

Mike continued singing, joined by the puberty-afflicted voices of the other boys, and our eyes met. The heat, the auditorium, the other people, all disappeared, and I was swimming in the blue of his eyes. His voice wrapped around me and grew above me, like a maze I wanted to explore.

Mike turned and the spell was broken. I bolted for the exit and didn't stop moving until ice-cold Coke was pouring down my throat as I tried in vain to douse the heat of a flame deep inside of me.

GROWING UP IOWA

When my family went on vacations and people found out I lived in Des Moines, their first comment was always, "Oh, so you live on a farm." I didn't. Des Moines was a city with several nice malls, large movie theaters, and most of the restaurants you had ever heard of, but our nightly news would feature stories like, "A man's wallet was stolen from his truck while he assisted an elderly lady across the street." Visitors from bigger cities would laugh at what was considered the breaking story, but we were just offended for the man whose wallet was stolen.

The 1970s and 80s were a good time to grow up in Iowa. People sipped lemonade on their porches and chatted with their neighbors in the evenings. When they had somewhere to go, they drove slowly, and a traffic jam meant you had to wait at the stoplight for more than one cycle. The parks were full of families picnicking and kids flying kites, and the front doors of the schools were propped open with rocks to let in the breeze.

It was not uncommon to see farmers in their muddy boots and overalls eating at the same diner as bankers and lawyers dressed in Italian suits. I knew any one of those farmers might have over a million dollars in his bank account. Or he might be so broke the bank had already started to foreclose on his house. Either way, he would not let you buy his lunch.

Kids were allowed, and even encouraged, to ride their bikes around their neighborhoods for endless hours without ever feeling the need for parental supervision. Then, one terrible day in 1982, a twelve-year-old paperboy was kidnapped while delivering papers in the early morning. The entire population of Des Moines was terrified and shocked. Mothers began driving their children down the street to play at a friend's house. Parents started accompanying their children on the walk to school, and the aimless bike riding came to an abrupt stop. The boy was never found. Even now, if you say his name to a long-term resident of Des Moines, you will hear the whole, sad story.

I felt comfortable in Des Moines. But at school things had always been different. Even as a young girl I studied my peers and concluded that I didn't fit in any group. For years, I watched girls walk the hallways at school or sit laughing in the bleachers during school basketball games, and I tried to figure out ways I might become part of those groups. Did a person just walk up and sit down with the people? Was it better to write one of the girls a note asking for permission to sit next to her? Nothing I came up with seemed likely to work.

But one day this problem was solved in a most unusual way.

It happened in eighth grade in the girls' bathroom at school. I assumed I had the bathroom to myself since I was there during the middle of class. I didn't see anyone when I walked in, and I was preoccupied with thoughts of nouns and verbs and dissecting sentences. My English teacher took her job seriously, and I thought that if teaching ever fell through for her, she should take a stab at being a prison warden.

"I heard Stacie is moving to Tennessee," a voice said to me as I washed my hands. It had taken me years to form a friendship with Stacie, and I was taking it pretty hard that she was moving away. The voice startled me, and I was at a loss as to who was speaking to me or how I should answer. I settled on silence.

"When she moves," the voice continued after my silence, "we should be friends."

The water had grown hot, and I finally noticed that my hands were turning bright red. I turned the faucet off, and when I looked up Lori was standing next to me expecting a response.

Unaccustomed to making friends in the girls' bathroom, I hesitated a few moments while my brain caught up with reality. I had been acquainted with Lori since second grade. She was funny, uninhibited, crazy, perfect.

"Okay," I finally answered.

"Good." She turned on her heel and walked away. She didn't say another word to me until a few months later when Stacie had packed and left. Stacie had been my best friend for two years. Her family moved away in the cold of December, and I sulked around wishing for Christmas to come faster because I've always loved the holiday season.

When it finally rolled around, Christmas morning was, indeed, magical. Our small family had a tradition of sleeping as late as we wanted instead of waking up early to open gifts like most of the other families we knew. My brother, Michael, was two years younger than me, and he was the last one to wake up. He stumbled into the kitchen in his Dallas Cowboys pajamas, sleep lines still crisscrossing his face. Christmas music was playing softly as Mom began warming the griddle to make the highly anticipated Swedish pancakes she had made every Christmas morning for as long as I could remember, and a sweet, delicious smell caused our stomachs to rumble.

Michael and I sat across from each other eating as many of the thin pancakes sprinkled with cinnamon and sugar as we could while Dad read about the birth of Jesus from the Bible. It was the one day of the year that Michael and I gladly helped clear the table and clean the dishes. By that point, we would have done anything in order to open our presents faster.

My favorite gift that year was a large, silver boom box. After Michael opened his last gift, a lamp with a Dallas Cowboy helmet as a lampshade, I gathered all my cassette tapes and lay wrapped in blankets on the floor with the boom box speakers near my head singing along with Depeche Mode. I felt giddy when the second side began playing automatically and I didn't need to remove the cassette and flip it manually. When side one began to play a second time, I ejected the tape and chose my new U2 tape and sang with Bono the lyrics of *Sunday Bloody Sunday* from my blanket cave. Then I listened to 'Til Tuesday and Duran Duran and Don Henley and when the phone rang I barely noticed it.

"Sharla, it's for you," Mom called after picking up on the twelfth ring.

"It is?" I asked. "Is it Grandma?"

Mom shook her head, focusing on a recipe she had started for something that smelled like garlic and butter, and handed me the phone.

"Hello?"

"Hi. It's Lori."

"Oh. Hi."

"Do you want to go to a movie?"

"When?"

"Now."

"Now? It's Christmas."

"I know. Do you want to go?"

"Did your mom say you could go?"

"Yeah. She'll drive us if you want to go."

"Okay … I'll ask."

Knowing there was no chance I'd be allowed to go anywhere on Christmas Day, I asked Mom anyway and felt light-headed when she said I could go. We went, and that was it. We were best friends. So I ended up getting Lori for Christmas.

THE BOY AGAIN

"I want you to meet my brother," Lori told me one day after school. It was early spring, and the increasing sun was coaxing tiny, green buds into replacing the snow on the tree branches. "He's picking me up, so walk with me down to the parking lot."

"That science test was easier than I thought it would be," I said as I shut my locker door and followed Lori down the steps of the school.

"Are you serious?" she asked. "It was terrible! I'm sure I failed."

"Oh." After four months of being friends with Lori, I had discovered that test taking was not something she excelled at. "You should try to retake it, and I'll help you study. It really wasn't very hard."

"Yeah, but instead of that, I think I'll just do nothing. I hate tests."

I rolled my eyes at her just as a clunky, white Nova pulled into the parking lot. Duct tape held the left headlight in place, and the loud muffler silenced the crowd of students waiting for their rides.

"There he is!" Lori pulled my elbow and steered me toward the Nova. "This is my brother."

Stunned, I stared in silence.

"Hi," Mike said, blond mane blowing in the breeze. "It's nice to meet you." I watched in a daze as he effortlessly grabbed Lori's heavy backpack and tossed it into the trunk.

"Can I drive home?" Lori asked sliding into the driver's seat.

"No, and don't turn the car off. It won't start."

"How did you get it started to come get me?"

"I have to open the hood and start it with a screwdriver."

"Can you teach me how to do that?"

He smiled and turned his head to pierce me with his blue eyes. "See you later, Sharla."

"Yeah," I whispered as he opened the driver's side door and made Lori get out.

"Mike is your brother?" I asked, grabbing her arm as she passed me on the way to the passenger door.

"Yeah, do you know him?" She looked confused.

"I saw him at camp, but I've never met him, and I didn't know he was related to you."

"Oh, good. Usually girls only want to be friends with me so they can meet Mike. I'm sick of it, so I'm glad you didn't know we were related."

She waved out the window as they drove away, and I tried to calm the thudding of my heart.

SCARY DOG

The first time I went to Lori's house, I almost ran away. We went after school, and when she began to unlock the door, she stopped and said, "My dog might scare you."

"Is it a big dog?" I asked.

"No. She's a small Boston terrier named Mugsy."

Boston terrier: a short-snouted breed between ten and twenty-five pounds. I wondered what could be scary about such a dog. Then Lori swung the door open, and a hideous creature ran toward us. Its face was completely flat and so black it would have been impossible to notice a nose or a mouth. The eyes, however, were alarmingly visible since they bulged out of their sockets to such a degree it appeared as if they might pop out and roll across the floor like eyeball marbles. Its tiny, stick legs looked incapable of supporting the snorting, round mass that ran toward us in a sideways limp. I tried to scream, but I was paralyzed in fear. Just as the creature was about to jump on me, Lori shouted, "Mugsy, down!"

"That is Mugsy?" My brain screamed. "That is a dog?" To my astonishment, Lori calmly walked across the room and tossed her backpack onto the table while the scary dog snorted at her heels.

"Hi, Mugsy." She bent and actually touched the thing. "Are you happy to see us?"

Still rooted to the same spot, I calmed myself. Upon closer inspection, I was willing to admit that this animal was a dog, but not like any dog I had ever seen before. I had seen squishy-nosed dogs. This was more like a warped nightmare creature.

She snorted constantly, which I figured was probably because her flat nose was doing her no good. Her bottom teeth stuck out more than a little, and her tail curled up like a pig's tail.

"Why does she run sideways?" I asked, finally able to speak.

"What do you mean?"

"She runs at you sideways. Like her head is barely in front of her tail. Why does she do that?"

"Oh. I guess I forgot that most dogs don't do that. She broke a couple legs when she was little, and she has walked weird ever since. Plus, I think she just gets going too fast to control herself." Lori had rolled the dog onto her back and was scratching her stomach while Mugsy snorted for more. "So, do you want a snack?"

And that was that. The scary dog went back to nap in front of the heating vent, and we ate chips. Although I tried not to touch the dog too often, fearing to be infected by the ugliness, I did grow used to her.

I decided that, although Mike fascinated me, I would not allow that to jeopardize my friendship with Lori. He was two years older than us, and, while friendly, he was usually busy with his own group of friends. I shoved Mike to the back of my mind and allowed my interest in him to simmer unobtrusively, until, eventually, it was nearly gone.

Lori was my best friend, and best friends can be tricky to find.

I can see how it would be nice, sometimes, to be surrounded by a crowd of people. Birthday parties and football games are more fun in a crowd, but, really, one good friend is all it takes to make it through the ups and downs of teenage life. It makes a world of difference to

tell your troubles to someone. It can literally be the difference between life and death.

Lori made that difference for me. She was on my side no matter
what, and it didn't even matter if I was right. She only listened to my
side of the story and never pointed out my faults. It was comforting.
The world has too few of these people. I wish I could give everyone
a Lori.

COLLEGE

When my parents waved good-bye and drove away after settling me into my dorm room at the University of Northern Iowa, it took every ounce of willpower I possessed to stand in the parking lot instead of running after them and begging them to take me home. Our family was small, and we were very close. I always felt safe and loved at home, and this new place felt unsettling.

I was starting college in January of 1990, one semester late. When all of my friends had gone away to college a semester earlier, I had gone to New Jersey to be a nanny. After only a few weeks, I knew that I hated being a nanny. The family I was living with was scary and mean, and I returned home as soon as I could. Then I found a job at a stationary store and worked from the middle of October until I was able to leave for college in January. After one failed attempt to move away from home, this new experience was unnerving.

I walked back into my dorm room and saw the curtains my mom had picked out and desk my dad had spent the afternoon assembling, and I threw myself onto my mattress and cried like a small child. My phone rang, but I decided not to answer it. After ten rings, I wrapped my pillow around my head. After twenty rings, I groaned and answered the phone.

"Hi," Lori said on the other end of the phone. "Let's go walk around campus and get something to eat."

"I'm not really hungry," I said, wiping my eyes.

"Then I'll eat and you can watch. Be there in five minutes."

As we walked around campus, Lori reoriented me. She introduced me to about a hundred people and had me belly laughing by suppertime.

I discovered that college was fun, people were everywhere, the science building felt like home to me, the studying was relentless, and, no matter how hungry I was, college food tasted like the sole of a tennis shoe.

LOVE DIES HARD

I walked into Lori's dorm room after having supper with my parents and grandparents, threw my geology books onto the bed, and grabbed a can of Cherry Coke. I had a hard test the next day, but my roommate and her boyfriend were in my dorm room, so, as was often the case, I found myself in Lori's room instead of my own.

"You're going to study now?" Lori asked. "*Friends* is on, and I was just about to watch it."

"Go ahead. I need to study, but the noise won't bother me," I told her. I sat down at her tiny desk and opened the enormous textbook to the correct chapter. "Thank you for being my friend and not having overly sensitive, easily hurt feelings."

"Who did you make cry now?" Lori asked as she plopped herself onto the bottom bunk, across from the television.

"Grandma."

"At least it wasn't your mom again. Remember when you told her that she got her feelings hurt too easily and that made her cry?"

"Which proved my point exactly," I said. "Which, by the way, is the wrong thing to say to someone who is crying."

"You told her that? While she was crying?" Lori looked at me, eyes wide.

"She was demonstrating proof of my hypothesis. How could I not mention that?"

"So what happened this time?" Lori asked, laughing.

"It started great. It was nice to see everyone, and I'm glad they came to visit. But while we were eating, my grandma said that if I ever have a daughter I should name her Sadie. I told her it sounded like an old lady's name. It turns out that her mother was named Sadie. She cried. I felt bad, which, as you know, turns my mind metallic and I start acting like a robot."

"Well, the week wouldn't be complete if you didn't hurt someone's feelings."

"I know. Why does this always happen?"

"I don't know. You never hurt my feelings. But you say things bluntly."

"I'm a scientist. We're blunt people."

"Didn't you know that your great-grandmother's name was Sadie?" Lori asked.

"Probably, but I wasn't thinking about that. However, I would like to point out that my hypothesis was again proved. Sadie is the name of my great-grandmother. So I was correct when I said it sounded like the name of an old lady."

"Do you think you and Rick will get married?" Lori asked, changing the subject in her usual sudden way. I had dated Rick through most of high school. He was two years older than me and two years into his studies at a university in Missouri. I shoved my geology work aside and thought about Lori's question. Lori and I were taking the class together, but while I was enthralled with the properties of hematite and was astounded that the mineral was found on the planet Mars, Lori could barely bring herself to open her textbook.

"I don't know," I mumbled, opening my can of Cherry Coke and taking a large gulp. "I can't imagine my life without Rick. He's been around so long he feels like a part of me."

"So, yes?" Lori asked, right eyebrow raised. It was the look she gave me when she wanted the truth instead of the first answer that popped into my mind.

I took a deep breath and glanced at the table of facts I was supposed to memorize about the crystal structure of minerals. "When I think about spending the rest of my days with Rick, I feel like an actress trying really hard to channel a role that no longer fits."

"I don't know what you mean by that."

"It just seems so … the same. When I'm with Rick, we are both the same as we used to be, and neither of us is who we are."

"You don't think he loves you?"

"I think he does love me in his way." I rubbed my forehead, willing my thoughts to straighten out and make sense. "I want to spend my life with someone who is amazing and makes me amazing. I don't want someone exactly like me, but I want us to be echoes of each other. Rick has changed, and I have changed, too. We think so differently from each other now, but when we are together we just fall into the same patterns that we've always had, even though they are false now.

"I want love to use me up until there is nothing left. I want love to be shocking. I'm in a relationship that feels like a soft quilt; it is always the same and never delightful or terrifying. And that feels soothing, but I'm worried that what I really want and what he really wants have very little to do with each other."

I called and broke up with him the next day. I spent the rest of the day panicking and crying. The day after that I called him, and we got back together. That weekend he came for a visit.

"You haven't changed very much since you graduated and moved away," he told me as we strolled across campus. Winter was nearly over, but a light dusting of snow had given the campus a fresh, clean appearance, and the stars were particularly dazzling in the crisp air.

"Did you expect me to?"

"Well, I changed a lot, and I've been kind of waiting because I thought the same thing would happen to you." He grabbed my hand in his and shoved both of them into his large coat pocket.

"I think I have actually changed, just not in the ways you were expecting. And I've been waiting for you to change back to who you used to be," I explained while the icy wind whipped my hair into my face.

"I'm not going to. I've grown up, and I can't believe the spiritual things you believe in," he picked up in the middle of our stressful and continual disagreement. "I can't pin our existence on a God there is no proof of, and I can't believe there is some great purpose for all of us. We are here because we are here, and that is all there is to it."

"But what about your dreams of traveling the world and helping people and all of that stuff you used to want to do with your life? Can you really give up on that?" Even though I knew what his answer would be, I couldn't help the tiny bit of hope inside me that still clung to a future in which we were united.

"There is really no reason to spend my life doing that, is there?" His sandy brown hair hung in front of his right eye and he blew it to the side. "I would only be doing it to feel good about myself, so even my good deeds would end up being selfish. I don't know what I am going to do. I'd love to just go somewhere other than America, rent a crummy little room, get to really know myself and find fulfillment in unexpected places. I don't know how you can still believe in all that stuff our parents taught us."

I breathed through the crack in my heart. "It's like a part of me, the most important part, is tethered to a spiritual reality that I know in my soul is true. I can ignore it, but I would be lying to myself because it's inside me, and I feel it. I am sure of it. As sure as I am of the warmth of your hand or the smell of your skin. To discount it would siphon the meaning out of life."

When I watched Rick drive away, I felt alarmingly hollow. I wondered if the piece of my heart he took with him was as real to him as it was to me. I wondered if he would see it, if he looked hard enough, on the seat next to him or find it in his coat pocket. I knew for sure that he had it because where it used to beat and thump inside my chest was now just dead space.

Although our relationship was clearly a dead end, I could not bear to make a clean break of it. We lived in a perpetual breakup until the connection between us finally snapped months later.

THE KISS

The first time Mike kissed me, I ran away. This was mostly because it altered my life as I knew it. Lori, Mike, and I were all in Des Moines over the summer, and Lori and I had made plans. I went to her house, but when I showed up Mike told me that Lori had left with her boyfriend. I wasn't surprised. Her boyfriend was getting ready to travel to Japan, and she wanted to be with him as much as possible.

"You can come inside, though, and hang out with me," Mike said. Since he was, quite literally, my only other college friend who had returned for the break besides Lori, I decided to go inside.

"I just made some popcorn and we can go eat it on the roof," Mike said, immediately causing me to regret my choice.

"The roof?" I sputtered.

"Sure."

"Of the house?"

"It's safe; don't worry," he nonchalantly assured me as he returned from the kitchen with a bowl of popcorn and a jug of apple juice.

"How do you plan on getting on the roof?" I asked, backing toward the door.

"I just climb out the upstairs bathroom window. It's easy."

"Um, first of all," I explained as I grabbed the doorknob, "I like to do my walking on the ground, and, second, I really like your parents and don't want to make them mad. So I think I'll just go home."

"Come on," he grabbed my hand and pulled me toward the steps leading upstairs. "It's fine."

After he assured me a hundred times that his parents would not hate me, I sighed, climbed the steps, and headed out of the window and onto the roof. I sucked my breath in and held it as the ground far below me began spinning. I shuffled my feet across the rough shingles until I reached Mike, who was sitting with his legs dangling off the edge. I gingerly sat next to him, pretending it was something I did every day, and, after a few moments, the world stopped whirling and settled down into its proper place.

The scent of warm shingles surrendered to the intoxicating perfume of lilac bushes in full bloom, and a blizzard of cotton puff from a cottonwood tree floated on the breeze – a white web across the green yards - as I watched from my perch on the roof. As the sun set, and with a bowl of popcorn between us, we talked. We compared our two colleges and told stories about our friends. I confessed I wasn't good at math and I unintentionally hurt people's feelings regularly, and he told me stories about driving a taxi in Minneapolis. He told me he had been threatened and even had a knife pulled on him.

"That's really scary," I said. "How do you deal with that?"

"It's my car, and I'm the boss," he explained. "Some people just need to be reminded of that. When the guy waved a knife at me, I slammed on my brakes in the middle of traffic and yelled at him to get out. He was so surprised he just obeyed. One time I realized I was witnessing a drug deal, so I just drove away. Three guys ran after me and climbed onto the car, but I just drove faster and they fell off. Another time a guy told me he didn't have any money to pay me, so I followed him into his apartment and he ended up paying me with a stereo."

I tried to reconcile the easygoing Mike I knew with the tough cabbie, and, oddly, it made sense.

"So," Mike said, "tell me one thing that you like about yourself."

"Sometimes I knowingly wear clothes that don't match," I said without thinking.

"Why?" he laughed.

"I don't know why I just told you that," I said. It had just slipped out, and I was sure he would think I was crazy.

"But you did." He grinned. "So you are obligated to answer my questions about it. Why do you do that? I mean, I don't match very often, but it's usually because I am unaware of the fact."

"I actually haven't thought very deeply about it." I took a deep breath and continued. "But when I choose to put on some ridiculous color combination, it makes me feel independent. Like I know what everybody wants me to do and I am choosing to do things my own way instead. I guess it is my own personal rebellion. It's weird."

"Yeah, I was just sitting here thinking how weird you look," he said quietly, an odd burning in his eyes. "I mean, your eyes are either blue or green, and I want to stare at them to figure out which one. And your hair is, like, thirty different colors of blond, which I didn't even know was possible. Weird."

I gulped and felt my cheeks redden as I tried to decide if he had intended to compliment me.

"What do you want to do after college?" he asked me, changing subjects.

"Well, I want to travel a lot." I sighed, relieved at the safer topic. "I want to see as much of the world as possible and then see it all again. What about you?"

"I want to help people. Probably high school kids. There is so much pressure in high school to be someone other than who we are, and I want to help kids who feel that way."

"Really?" My hand brushed his as I reached for some popcorn, and a sizzling jolt of lightning shot up my arm and directly into my heart.

"You sound surprised."

"No. It's just really great that you want to do something like that. Do you think you will be a teacher or something?"

"No, I want to be a youth pastor. For me, it would be useless to do anything to try to help kids without bringing the spiritual element into it. My faith has been a rock for me, and I can't imagine trying to ignore it." He glanced, almost shyly, at me. "I know it might sound weird, and I know there are a lot of great ways to help kids. But, for me, everything I really am flows out of my spiritual life."

"I think that's great," I whispered, remembering the conversation that ended my relationship with Rick. "I've always known that there is a deep well of the spiritual inside of me, and to try to ignore it seems empty and shallow."

"I also want to get married and have about ten kids," he announced, throwing some popcorn into his mouth.

"Ten? Do you hate peace and quiet?"

"I love kids."

"You really want ten?" I asked, amazed.

"Yeah. I mean, I guess I would settle for eight or nine, but I really love kids. What about you?"

"I'm not sure being a mom is really something I would excel at. It is one of those all-or-nothing things. It's overwhelming," I said, swatting at a mosquito.

"Really? You would be a great mother."

"Why aren't you being eaten alive by mosquitoes like I am?"

"They never bite me. I don't even remember ever having a mosquito bite."

"That is completely unfair and makes me hate you."

He laughed. "You want to go inside and watch a movie?"

"Sure, but you might have to airlift me off this roof."

"You can do it." He smiled. "It gets better after you actually move."

"Actually moving is the problem," I confessed. The ground had begun to spin violently again, and my heart was beating in a panic.

"I'll help you." Mike laughed as he grabbed my elbow. Once I was up he grabbed my cold, trembling hand in his, and the warm sensation captured my attention. As we walked across the roof, I thought only of my hand in his and not once about the twirling ground.

We drank apple juice and ate Cheetos and ended up laughing and telling stories long after the movie was over. As we talked, we moved closer and closer until my arm brushed against his at the slightest movement.

I knew he was going to kiss me ten seconds before it happened. In that space of time, everything I had done, said, and experienced collided with all that was yet to be. The whole of my identity, past, present, and future, swirled together, blending and condensing until all of it became a tiny point of reality resting inside one moment of time.

The second Mike kissed me my world shifted. Something that felt like electric tingles raced from my lips to my toes, and a burning filled my entire body. I completely ceased breathing, and my heart paused until I thought I would surely die and then made up for its inactivity with a staccato hammering I was positive he could hear. I had an intense desire to wrap myself around him and kiss him for the next several hours, but before I could even make a proper response, I was filled with alarm - I was kissing my best friend's brother. The shock violently ripped through my mind until there was only one thing I could do. Run.

I turned and dashed to Lori's room, climbed into her bed, and waited for her to come home. She returned very late, and a deep sleep had already overtaken me eliminating the need to talk to her about the experience of kissing her brother, an anomaly I couldn't explain—even to myself.

I thought that running away and falling asleep would cover up the accidental kiss, and we could both pretend it had never happened and just go on like before. However, the memory of it kept popping into my mind at inconvenient times, like during church or supper with the family. Or in my dreams at night. It wasn't just a kiss; it was a moment that changed everything.

I assumed Mike was trying to ignore the kiss as much as I was, but the next time I saw him he took me aside and apologized for taking me off guard. I didn't want to talk about it much since I had not yet explained to myself how I felt about the experience, so I just mumbled something, smiled, and walked away. Years later, I discovered that he had apologized due to utter confusion. Apparently, my reaction didn't make much sense to him.

When I returned to school after the summer break, I breathed a sigh of relief and embraced my studies, vowing to achieve excellent grades. Lori and I had moved into an apartment together, and one evening Mike called.

"Here," Lori said, holding the phone in my direction. "Mike wants to talk to you."

"Really?" I asked. "Why would he want to talk to me? We're just acquaintances."

"I didn't ask him why. Just take the phone," Lori told me.

"Hello?"

"We're just acquaintances?" Mike asked, angrily. "We've known each other since junior high, you ate popcorn on my roof, and we shared a pretty incredible kiss. Does that sound like an acquaintance?"

"Um." My mind turned to metal and I froze.

"She's sorry," Lori shouted from across the room, where she was able to clearly hear her brother's elevated voice. "She just talks that way."

I spoke robotically through the rest of the conversation and laughed nervously before saying good-bye.

"Thanks for getting me out of that," I said to Lori, as I hung up the phone.

"You guys kissed?" she asked.

"Um," I uttered as a cold, metallic sensation froze my mind.

DATING GAME

"How was your date?" Lori asked as I caught our crazy cat, Fred, before he landed on my face. We had adopted him from the rescue league when we moved in together. As soon as the key turned the lock in our front door, Fred would launch himself through the air and we would catch a brief glimpse of a flying cat before he landed on one of us. He woke me up in the mornings by chewing my eyelashes. When your first vision of the day is a mouth descending on your eyeball, it can be frightening.

I shut the apartment door and threw my purse onto the gold couch we had purchased from Goodwill. "Well, it's nine o'clock and I'm already home. That about says it all."

"Maybe you just don't want it to work out with anyone because you're still so upset about Rick?"

"No. I think all guys want to do is drink beer and be jerks."

"Oh. Clearly, I was wrong."

I threw Fred at her and smiled when she caught him with one hand and tucked him under her arm with the practiced skill of someone who had perfected this maneuver. Fred meowed, content in his warm nest.

"I think Fred needs a bath," I said as I washed my hands. "He smells."

"He got stuck in the trash can again," she explained.

"Maybe we should leave the lid off."

"Maybe you shouldn't make it impossible for me to set you up with someone."

"It might help if you would set me up with a boy who is actually nice."

"What about Dave?"

"True, he was nice. His girlfriend thought so, too."

"Good point. Chad?"

"Showed up drunk."

"Steve?"

"Full of himself."

"William?"

"Womanizer."

"Brad?"

"Needy."

"You should just date my brother."

"Never!"

"You are perfect for each other."

"We would never work, and I don't like him."

"Then why are your cheeks red?"

I turned away and felt my cheeks; they were burning. Lori might have said more, but I couldn't hear her over the pounding of my heart.

Weeks later, when she mentioned for a second time that I should date her brother, I wondered if she was testing our friendship. I remembered all the girls who had used friendship with Lori as a way to get noticed by Mike. I remembered Lori's reaction, which was one of intense resentment and eternal shunning.

The third time she made herself clearer by telling me, "You're perfect for him, dummy." I thought again about Mike. I wondered if we were perfect for each other.

I thought about my astronomy teacher and how he had said that stars are total absorbers because any object—a rock, ice, or even radiation—that travels near the star becomes engulfed in its brilliance.

The star absorbs the matter or energy and then shines all the more brightly. I couldn't help, though, the anxiety that rippled down my spine as I worried about the object that became engulfed in a reality not its own.

I wondered if Mike would absorb me.

I wondered if he already had.

The violent storm blew open Lori's front door and ushered in a vortex of snow and a husky. The second semester of my freshman year was over, and, since I was a semester behind everyone my age, I would begin the first semester of my sophomore year in January. We were spending Christmas break at Lori's house in Des Moines numbing our brain cells with television and junk food. We were in the middle of a movie marathon after being snowed out of all our other options.

"Where did you get that dog?" Lori asked Mike, who followed the husky through the doorway.

"I found him in the middle of the road just after I got to Des Moines," Mike explained as he shook the snow from his hair and shut the door against the cold. He was attending a college in Minneapolis and had just arrived home. "I was driving slowly because it's almost impossible to see anything with this thick snow. Then, I noticed the gleam of his eyes, so I opened my car door and he just jumped in."

"He is gorgeous," I said cautiously holding out my hand to let the dog get used to me. "His eyes are ice blue."

"I know," Mike said. "I'm gonna keep him."

"Is he friendly?" Lori asked.

"Yeah," Mike assured us. "I already took him to the park and we played and wrestled."

"In this blizzard?" I asked, looking out the window at the white neighborhood. The snow lent a deceptive brightness to the night, and covered the damage of the season with its clean, quiet blanket. The topography of the front yard had disappeared under a flat illusion, and the houses across the street were impossible to discern due to the curtain of giant snowflakes.

"He loves the snow," Mike said, laughing as the dog jumped onto its hind feet and licked Mike across the cheek. "I made snowballs, and he chased them. He tried to bring them back to me but always ended up eating them. Besides, I had to make sure he was friendly before I brought him around anyone."

"Um, were you walking barefoot in the snow?" I asked, looking at his red feet.

"I do it all the time. I don't get cold."

"But, it's literally freezing. You have to be cold. If skin is exposed to a temperature near the freezing point for more than a few minutes, you won't just feel cold, you will actually begin to freeze."

"Nope," he said as he walked into the kitchen searching for food for the dog.

Buddy, named so by Mike because of his friendliness, followed Mike like a shadow for the next three weeks. Buddy slept in Mike's bed, rode shotgun in Mike's car, and sat next to him on the couch, like a human, and watched television.

"That dog loves you like crazy," I told Mike when I stopped by his and Lori's house. Mike was lying on the living room floor propped on his elbows reading a book with Buddy plastered against him like a sock on a sweatshirt just out of the dryer. Buddy thumped his tail in greeting and then fell back asleep with his head resting on Mike's shoulder.

"He's the best dog in the world," Mike said as he reached around and scratched Buddy's ear.

"What are you going to do with him when you go back to college?" I asked.

"I don't know," Mike said. "I keep thinking that I could just sneak him into my dorm room and nobody would have to know about him. He's really quiet."

"Yeah," I said. "But he's also huge. I think he'd be rather noticeable. Especially since he looks like a wolf. That might cause a stir."

"I know," he admitted. "But he'd be great to have with me when I drive cab. Nobody would mess with me after seeing him sitting in the front seat."

"Are you still trying to figure out how to take Buddy to college?" Lori asked as she plopped into an overstuffed chair and swung her legs over the armrest. "I say you do it. He's so friendly. Also, you should come to UNI with us. It would be fun, and it's so much cheaper than what you are paying."

But two days before Mike was scheduled to return to Minneapolis, he threw himself into a kitchen chair and slammed a crumpled piece of paper onto the table.

"Oh no," I said as I smoothed out the paper. Buddy's face stared back from the center of the paper with a phone number under his picture.

"I looked at the lost dog ads in the paper for two weeks, and nothing about Buddy was in there that whole time."

"What are you going to do?" Lori whispered.

"I don't know," Mike moaned. "Who would wait three weeks before advertising for a lost dog?"

"I'm sorry, Mike," I whispered. Buddy bolted in from the backyard like his tail was on fire and jumped onto Mike's lap, squeezing himself into the small space between Mike and the kitchen table. Mike wrapped his man-sized arms around his dog and buried his face in Buddy's fur like a little boy.

Feeling helpless, Lori and I left them in the kitchen. I knew it would break Mike's heart to be separated from Buddy, and I suspected it would break the dog's heart, too. I had rarely seen such a powerful connection as the love between those two.

The next day Mike made his decision.

"I have to give the dog back," he announced. "I'm really tempted to keep him, but I can't keep a dog for myself if some kids love and miss him. It's the right thing to do."

Mike told me later that when Buddy saw his owner, he whined and hung his head, refusing to leave Mike's side. The owner, belly swelled beyond the capacity of his shirt buttons, shouted at the dog for running away and smacked him hard on the nose with a stick, opening Buddy's skin so that blood stained his white fur. Mike reached for Buddy to grab him back, but the owner yanked Buddy away and heaved him into the back of his dilapidated pickup truck. Mike called Buddy back to him, but the owner was surprisingly quick and drove away.

Mike ran after the truck, calling to Buddy, but Buddy just stared, tail down, until Mike could no longer keep pace and Buddy was gone. Mike drove around the neighborhood for hours trying to locate the old truck and calling Buddy's name, but he never found them. He called the police and reported animal cruelty, but he didn't have enough information for the police to do anything.

Mike missed the first day of the semester and stayed in town driving from morning until night trying to find Buddy. He thought he saw the truck one time, and he followed it until it pulled into a driveway and an elderly man climbed out. Even though it was not the same man, Mike yelled for Buddy until his voice grew hoarse. But Buddy was gone.

UPON A MOTORCYCLE

L ori had pestered Mike about attending the University of Northern Iowa with us, and, probably in large part due to his broken heart over Buddy, he actually agreed. He was late to return to Minneapolis after searching for the dog, and our semester started one week later than the college he had attended. So, that January, we all headed to Cedar Falls together.

I told myself this would not be a problem. We were both mature people and, for Lori's sake, we could certainly overcome what had happened over the summer.

I blame what transpired on Lori. Mike ended up living in a tiny dorm room with two international students, Carlos from Costa Rica and Jin from Korea. Lori felt bad that her brother was so cramped in his tiny dorm room, so she continually invited him over. We had a nice-sized apartment with a full kitchen, which we only really used for my chemistry experiments. Lori had learned never to drink from a glass full of liquid she had not poured herself, a hydrochloric acid spill had melted a section of the linoleum and ensured that we would never get our deposit back, and the cupboards held more beakers than dishes.

I don't think Lori intentionally ditched us. I think she was a typical college kid who made plans and then forgot them and made other plans. But, due to her, Mike and I spent most of the semester with just the two of us and the memory of a life-altering kiss.

I was taking an accelerated chemistry class in which chemistry one and two were offered together in one semester, and it was my hardest and favorite class. My teacher never combed his hair and rarely had all the buttons on his shirt fastened. He blew things up regularly, and on one occasion, he concocted a powerful potion that knocked him unconscious and caused the evacuation of the building. He had to be carried out on a stretcher. At that moment he became my favorite teacher ever.

We had a daunting test approaching, and I needed to do well. I enjoyed mixing chemicals and studying reactions, but the math, of which there was a great deal, was a great torment. I was giving my textbook a stare-down struggling to balance an equation when I heard a knock. I chased Fred and held him in the crook of my arm to spare the person on the other side of the door the shock of a flying cat landing on his or her face. When I opened the door, Mike was smiling and holding a pair of sunglasses in his hands.

"Hey, what are you doing?" he asked as I gazed at his brilliant smile.

"Studying for a chemistry test that is going to boss me around tomorrow."

"Sounds important, but how about ditching it and going on a motorcycle ride with me? It's a glorious spring day, and there is no better way to enjoy the sunshine than from the back of a motorcycle." I knew I needed to study, but I had never been on a motorcycle before, and I was helpless against Mike's smile.

"Grab some sunglasses," he told me. "It keeps the bugs out of your eyes."

As I got onto the back of the motorcycle, my heart began racing.

"You're going to have to hold on to me," Mike said over his shoulder.

Not sure of the proper way to hold on, I gingerly grabbed onto his waist.

SHARLA HINTZ

"Like this," he laughed and grabbed my hands stretching my arms around him so I was hugging his back.

"Oh." The word came out more as a breath.

He started the motorcycle, and the ground raced out from underneath us. As I watched the world speed by, hugging Mike tightly was no problem. In fact, after a couple miles, my muscles began to ache from intense clinging, and I forced myself to loosen my death grip. The air hit my face with such force I struggled to breathe.

My heart nearly stopped whenever we rounded a corner. The sensation of leaning toward the concrete while racing along at a blinding fifteen miles per hour was very disorienting, and I squeezed Mike and buried my face between his shoulder blades. His familiar sunshine-and-grass scent filled my lungs and nothing else mattered. I was alone with Mike in our own motorcycle reality where it was okay to hold onto him and not let go. I was happy.

"I was thinking," Mike said over his shoulder, "that we should stop at this pond up here."

"Okay," I said, looking around for the first time. We had been driving for some time, but I was only just realizing we were in a housing community that was in various stages of being built. The houses all looked large, and, someday this neighborhood would be full of fancy cars sitting in driveways and families who protected their homes with security systems.

I looked into the shell of a five bedroom house and imagined big-screen television sets, kids coloring at the island in the kitchen, and a dog in the backyard barking at the birds taking baths in the pond. The family who moved into this large, elegant house would not know that we had been here first. I felt excited and intrigued, like I was witnessing the beginning of something and I had no idea where the story would lead.

"How do you like riding a motorcycle?" Mike asked as I pried my clenched thighs off the seat.

"It freaks me out when the center of gravity changes."

"What?"

"When we turn a corner and lean toward the ground. The center of gravity changes. I don't like it."

"That's how you turn a motorcycle."

"I know. You shift the mass so the centrifugal force keeps the motorcycle upright. It's the right thing to do, but it feels disorienting."

"The girls are always saying that to me," Mike said with a shake of his head. "Let's go swimming."

"Where?"

"In the pond."

"What? We can't. It's a private pond."

"Not yet. Nobody lives here yet, so it seems pretty public to me." His blue-fire eyes flamed brightly, and I was lost to all reason.

"Okay." I giggled like a junior-high-school girl as I bent to remove my sandals. Just when I got the second shoe off, I felt the world fly by as Mike picked me up and tossed me into the freezing water. I felt him cannonball into the water next to me as I raced for the surface and gasped in mouthfuls of air.

"That was not necessary!" I shouted.

"But it was fun!"

"It's so cold. I can barely breathe."

"That's why I threw you in. I knew you wouldn't get in once you felt how cold the water is."

"Have you been here before?"

"No, but the temperature is pretty low at night, so I knew the water would be cold."

"I can't feel my toes."

"Really?"

"Not really, but it is freezing."

"Swim around faster and you'll warm up. Here, I'll help," he offered as he dunked my head below water.

"How does that help?" I sputtered after swimming as quickly as possible to the surface.

"It made you swim harder," He laughed.

"Oh. Here, I'll help you too." I swam after him, fully intending to dunk him as far as my arms would reach, but he was a much stronger swimmer than I was and escaped my grasp. After multiple attempts, I gave up and gazed at the nearly dark sky while floating on my back.

"Giving up?"

"I need to return to a normal rate of breathing," I explained.

"Admit it. You can't catch me."

"I could totally catch you if I wanted to," I lied, "but my T-shirt is slowing me down. It's heavy."

"I have a T-shirt on too."

"Mine is heavier," I said, eyes narrowed daring him to disagree.

"Well, in that case, let me escort you to the shore before your super heavy T-shirt drags you under. I had no idea how much danger you were in." Laughing, he wrapped his arm around my back and began swimming toward shore.

Finally on shore, we fell onto our backs, shoulders touching, and stared in silence at the first stars as they popped into existence.

"Beautiful, isn't it?" Mike asked in a quiet, almost reverent, voice. There were no lights to dim the brilliance of the constellations that soon lit up the sky, and the sight was mesmerizing.

"Yeah." I turned to discover my face only inches from his, all the passion of the blue flame suddenly evident in his eyes. He looked at my lips, and I knew he was going to kiss me. My heart thundered, and I wondered if I would stop him or kiss him back. With the slowest possible movements, he inched toward me, and my moment of decision had come. But then, a blindingly bright light streaked across the sky, and we both looked up to witness the most glorious falling star I had ever seen. If I didn't know better I would have sworn that we were in danger of being scorched by it.

"Wow!" Mike said. "I've never seen anything like that, and I've seen a lot of falling stars."

"A falling star is not really a star but actually a meteoroid entering the atmosphere," I said, shivering from the wet clothes and the cool night air. I breathed shallowly and wondered to myself if the beautiful light had been a sign, and, if so, what it meant.

"We should get back." Mike stood and helped me up. "I can hear your teeth chattering."

As much as I wanted to stay longer, I couldn't disagree. I had almost never felt colder, but, sitting on the back of his motorcycle with my face pressed between his shoulder blades and his scent in my lungs, I couldn't have been happier.

Before long my eyes were all a-twinkle, and my head was fuzzy. My grades were sinking, I put the cheese in the silverware drawer, and I put the peanut butter in the freezer; I turned off the bathroom light during Lori's shower. Since she is not stupid, Lori figured it out.

"You're in love with my brother," Lori said smugly across the pile of oceanography notes I was supposed to be studying.

"What? No," I said, intently studying the chemical composition of oceanic water.

"Yep, you are. It's obvious."

"No," I brilliantly refuted.

"You should just admit it. You guys are perfect for each other, and if you end up married, we would be sisters. He's coming over in a few minutes, but I'm gonna go buy some ice cream." Lori never studied long. She had a physical inability to focus on anything written down for longer than ten minutes.

"Be right back," she called over her shoulder. Before she shut the door Mike's voice floated through the doorway and into my living room. My knees went woozy.

THE DATE

"It's not an official date," I told Lori. "We are just going on a picnic."

"Whatever," she rolled her eyes.

We seldom left the college campus, so intentionally going somewhere together on an outing that was planned in advance was a big deal, but I was pretending that it wasn't.

It was an unseasonably warm day in April, and everyone wanted to be outside. There weren't many things that could compare with the colors that Iowa produced in the springtime. The tree farms, cornfields, prairies, and rolling hills showed off a hundred shades of green. The air was full of health, and I always got the feeling that a deep breath a day would keep the doctor away just as effectively as an apple.

Mike drove us in a friend's car to a park I had never been to before. He spread a blanket on the soft grass and laid out a delicious lunch of peanut butter and jelly sandwiches, Pringles with cheese in a squirt can, and Cherry Coke. As we ate I felt like I was in a movie. The sun sparkled brilliantly, and the sky was the perfect shade of blue. We talked about our dreams and complained about our teachers. I told him that the formation of volcanoes intrigued me, and he told me that he still missed Buddy.

Just when I thought we would pack our stuff and leave, Mike pulled out a Ninja Turtle kite. I loved it. The wind was strong, and we flew the kite for at least an hour, which was thrilling, but I really just liked holding the string together so our hands could touch. It gave me shivers that raced to my stomach and made me feel melty.

"Do you want to go for a walk?" Mike asked as he packed the kite and the blanket.

"Sure." I was excited to spend more time together. It had been a perfect afternoon, and I didn't want it to end.

We walked toward a creek, and he grabbed my hand, which immediately made my knees go weak. I stumbled, and he held my hand tighter. It was wonderful. We approached the creek, and, to my surprise, Mike walked right into the water, shoes and all.

"Come on in," he called since I had stopped where it was dry. "The water feels great."

"Okay," I laughed. Even though the water was actually quite frigid, I joined him in the creek, thankful that my sandals were somewhat water resistant. I was rewarded when I reached his side because he grabbed my hand again, and we continued walking.

"It's weird how creeks and rivers aren't straight but meander through the ground," Mike said, pointing ahead to the crazy back and forth bends in the creek bed.

"That happens," I explained, "because obstacles on one side of the bed or the other inhibit the rate at which the water flows causing the opposite side to increase in speed and cut into the earth … why are you looking at me like that?"

"I think you are perfect."

"What?" I laughed. "You're joking around."

"I'm not joking; it's true. You see the world as a beautiful mystery that needs solved. You've investigated and have a specific scientific answer to its uniqueness. It shouldn't surprise me anymore, but it does. I love the way your mind works. But it's more than just that." He walked to the side of the creek and shoved aside a large rock. When he turned back to me, he was holding a red rose.

"Roses are usually given as a sign of affection, but they're not my favorite flower," I whispered, even though a small voice in the back of my mind warned that, while true, this particular response was not appropriate.

With a small smile, he led me forward a few more steps, and suddenly he was handing me a second rose that I had not previously seen.

"Daisies are your favorite." He laughed. "But this is symbolic."

"I like roses more than carnations, which are my least favorite flower," I said as I fought against the metal that threatened to overtake my mind. A voice in the back of my head shouted at me to smile and stay calm. And silent.

"It's symbolic." He laughed again, handing me a magically appearing third rose. "Roses symbolize love, and thorns symbolize beauty that must be earned. You have some thorns," he said handing the flower to me, "but that makes your beauty even sweeter."

Finally obeying the voice of social wisdom, I smiled and said nothing, but the beating of my heart seemed loud enough to communicate through my silence. Every few steps he produced a rose, which he had previously hidden behind rocks or under clumps of grass, until we reached the edge of the park, and I had eleven roses.

Producing the twelfth rose from behind a mound of grass, he said, "You are the love of my life. My soul mate."

Sometimes love is like a sudden and fierce wildfire. It burns powerfully, unpredictably, and beautifully, and, whether you wish to be or not, you are scorched. Your reality has been shockingly changed; in fact, you, in the depths of your being, have been changed, and nothing is ever the same again. And while everything looks different, nothing is safe, and you haven't the slightest clue what you should do, you raise your head to the sky and thank God for the fire you know you can no longer live without.

He had patiently and gently broken through my analytical defense and touched my heart. I felt fierce passion and was surprised when my eyes filled with tears. He used the last rose to wipe a tear from my cheek, but I forgot about the roses and smashed them be-tween us as I rushed into his arms and gave him my heart.

⚓

Mike never told me anything was impossible. Even when I told him that after graduating I'd like to move to Alaska and live off the land, he listened as if this absurd notion was a real possibility. He never mentioned that I had so little experience living in the wild that I could probably not even survive a weekend camping trip without making a visit to Walmart. He didn't bring up wild animals, freezing temperatures, and mountains of pure ice. Any idea was worth talking about, and I loved him for it.

He made me feel like a whole world of possibilities lay just outside of my front door, and I wanted to try them all.

My grades had begun to suffer the consequences of too many mo-torcycle rides. Most of April had been unseasonably sunny, and the allure of being outside had been too strong to resist. However, finals were approaching at the end of May, and I was making a renewed at-tempt to focus.

"You know," he said over a pile of books in our usual booth at the student center, "if you're going to have half of these adventures, you'll need to learn to fish."

"Why would I need to fish?"

"It's a good way to obtain food, and I love fishing. So, there, you have two good reasons."

"Okay. But I don't think I will like it. I don't see the appeal."

"Don't see the appeal? What is not appealing about fishing? It is peaceful and quiet—man against nature. I can't think of many things I'd rather be doing. Plus, fish provide great protein that you may need when food options aren't available."

"I get the point about eating fish as a way of staying alive, but I don't see the point of recreational fishing. It seems quite boring and mean to me."

"Boring and mean? That is it. I am taking you fishing this Saturday when we go back to Des Moines."

"But, I'll feel so mean."

"It is mean. Mean that nobody took you fishing before this. Trust me," he said and looked straight into my eyes, "you'll love it."

"Okay." I was helpless when he looked at me like that.

FISHING

During college, Mike spent his summers working at a marina at Big Creek State Park giving sailing lessons and renting out boats. It was a forty-five-minute drive from my parents' house, so he arrived just before the sun rose Saturday morning.

"Any sport that involves waking up with the sun cannot be considered a fun activity," I complained, rubbing my eyes. Not a morning person, I had woken up fifteen minutes before Mike arrived, which allowed me barely enough time to brush my teeth, pull my hair into a ponytail, and shrug on whatever clothes were nearest to me.

"Well, good morning, Sunshine!"

"You aren't one of those people who loves mornings are you? Because if you start chattering and singing, I am going to get annoyed. Consider that a warning."

Mike laughed. "I have to be a morning person. I have to be at work before dawn all summer long. But don't worry. I'm used to working with fishermen, so I can handle your gruffness."

He opened the passenger door, and I sank into the seat wishing it were a mattress with blankets. I let him do most of the talking, but when we drove through the entrance of the state park, the first thing I saw was a dark orange ball just pushing itself up from the watery horizon. The water was glass-like in its stillness and perfectly reflected the deep, fiery colors that filled the sky. The air was thick with the smell of foliage, and trees that were older than my great-grandpa dominated the landscape, reaching toward heaven as if they might actually touch it. This beautiful place appeared to exist solely for the two of us. For the first time I recognized the allure of the small hours of the morning.

As we neared the marina, I noticed a couple trucks and a man carrying about twenty lifejackets walking toward a row of fishing boats.

"That old rusted truck over there," Mike explained, "belongs to a guy named Don. He's a schoolteacher, but he comes out here every day as soon as the weather is nice enough. I don't know how he makes it through the school year, but he will be drunk the entire summer. Hey, Mark!" he called to the man covered in lifejackets.

"Hey, Mike," Mark called as he tossed two lifejackets into a boat. "You working today?"

"No, Eric is coming in later."

"Do you work with him?" I asked as Mark turned to shove a fishing boat into the water and tie it to the dock.

"I work *for* him. He's my boss."

"And he doesn't know if you're working today?"

"He never knows who's working. He leaves it up to us to figure out. As long as all the days are covered, he doesn't really care."

"Looks like it's gonna be a nice day out here," Mike said to Mark as the last lifejacket was delivered.

"Yeah, I already have the boats all reserved, so business should be good. Don was out here before me this morning. He'll be drunk by noon, so that could get ugly."

"He never fails to excite." Mike put his arm around my waist, "This is Sharla, and I am going to teach her to fish today."

"Hello," Mark said. "Do you two want to take out a boat?"

"Don't you have them all reserved?" Mike asked Mark.

"Yeah, but if you want one go ahead and take it."

"No, that's okay. I'm taking her somewhere we need to walk to," Mike said.

"Okay. Do you want to take some chips or Gatorade with you?"

"No, thanks. We've got everything we need."

"All right. Have a fun time, kids," Mark called over his shoulder as he walked toward the paddle boats.

"Would he really have given us a boat even though they're reserved?" I asked as we walked away from the boats and toward a patch of forest.

"Yeah. Mark's funny that way. He doesn't always care if he makes people mad."

Mike grabbed my hand and directed me to a tiny path that wound its way through the dense trees. The leaves formed a canopy over our heads and the loamy scented air was thick and cool. When we finally reached the water, I stared, astonished at the breathtaking view. The golden sun floated just above the horizon, and the sky was filled with red, pink, and purple.

Before I could tear my gaze away, Mike placed a fishing pole in my hand and began showing me how to cast. I was no good at it, and it took several tries before the bait landed in the water instead of plopping onto the ground directly in front of us. We fished for a while, and when I got the hang of it, Mike gave me a different pole. I had no difficulty casting that one and watched proudly as the line flew to the center of the cove.

"Go ahead and reel it in," Mike said.

"Already?"

"Yeah. I think you caught something."

"Oh. I didn't see the bobber go under." I began reeling, but I didn't feel the tugging Mike had told me to expect if a fish had been hooked. "It doesn't feel like anything is on there," I told him.

"Just check," he told me.

"See," I said disappointed when the hook popped out of the water empty, "I didn't catch anything."

"I think you did," he persisted.

"Well, you know more about fishing than I do, but I don't see a fish on the end of the line."

"What do you see?"

"Just the hook."

"Are you sure?"

I raised an eyebrow at him skeptically, but I kept my thoughts to myself as I obediently reeled the line in the rest of the way. As the hook got closer, I took a second look and noticed it was not really a hook at all, but more of a circle. A golden circle.

I watched in silence as Mike grabbed the line and broke it, bent onto one knee, and said, "If we spend every day together from now until we die, I will only be sad that there are not more days to spend with you. Will you marry me?"

I blinked to make sure I hadn't slipped into a dream. Then I grew dizzy, which reminded me to breathe. I said something robotic that didn't come out as any recognizable word, and then I began to laugh. I fought the metallic sensation in my mind and told myself to say something.

"Yes!" I cried, lowering to my knees so I could wrap my arms around his neck, "I would love to marry you!"

He slipped the golden ring with diamonds in the shape of a flower onto my finger, and even the glorious sunrise could not tempt me to tear my eyes from it.

Lori was ecstatic that we were going to be sisters-in-law, and I could not believe how perfect my life had become.

TOO BLUNT

"You made my mom cry," Mike told me as we drove to Wal-Mart to pick up some last-minute supplies. We had used summer break to plan our wedding, but I took the next semester off school as well, and we were married in October. Nearly a year after our wedding we decided to put everything on hold and embrace our dream of traveling to Alaska. It was the eve of embarking on our adventure, and we were frantically packing as well as saying our good-byes to friends and family.

"I thought so," I groaned. The family had been sitting in the living room remembering our wedding as well as Mike's older brother's wedding. Mike's sister-in-law had made a statement that she would not change a thing about her wedding. I thought about my wedding a moment, and while I loved it all, the rehearsal dinner popped into my mind. My idea had been to have a friend, who was studying to be a chef, grill steaks and serve everyone at the church. I had intended it to be a simple and stress-free gathering of close friends. However, I didn't consider that someone would need to do all the setting of tables, washing of dishes, and cleaning up afterward. Of course, our parents were the ones who ended up performing these thankless jobs. I hadn't planned that very well. My informal and simple dinner turned out to be a lot of work for my parents and Mike's parents.

"There's just one thing I would change," I had said after all those thoughts sped through my mind.

"What?" someone asked.

"My rehearsal dinner," I said, believing it was a nice sentiment. Not offensive. And then I saw the stunned faces. Everyone slowly turned and looked toward Mike's mom, and her face fell. Her cheeks turned dark red, and she walked out of the room.

I searched my mind trying to figure out what had gone wrong and quickly realized that Mike's parents had been responsible for the rehearsal dinner. That was their contribution. I had planned it, but they had paid for it. Because my critique of it was in the planning, which I had done, it didn't occur to me that it would upset anyone.

Tension gripped me and all my thoughts turned metallic. Mike had followed his mom into the kitchen and eventually conversation in the living room resumed. I sat like a robot whose power switch had been flipped off until Mike grabbed my hand, and we left a short while later.

"I didn't think what I said would be upsetting because the part I would change was something I had overlooked in my planning. It had nothing to do with your mom," I tried to explain as Mike parked our small truck.

"I understand, but you didn't clarify that. You just said that you would change it. And it was her only contribution."

"I hate how this always happens." I groaned, rubbing my face with my hands. "Sometimes I feel like I should write down everything I'm about to say and have someone proofread it."

"I knew what you meant, so I explained it. I think it is okay now." Mike sighed. "You are pretty blunt sometimes."

"I've heard that before."

ALASKAN ADVENTURE

Early the next morning, with all of our possessions in the back of a small pickup, we drove north. As soon as we crossed the border into Canada, we felt the changes. The speed limit signs suddenly read one hundred, which made us excited until we realized it was referring to kilometers per hour instead of miles per hour. We ate at McDonald's and discovered that Canadian ketchup tasted vastly different from the ketchup we were used to. Canada smelled like snow and pine and looked like a sea of smiles.

We stayed for a while with Lori, who had married shortly after we had and had temporarily moved to Calgary with her Canadian husband. I had missed her terribly and was elated to see her again.

Then we loaded ourselves back into the compact pickup and resumed our adventure on the Alcan Highway. As Calgary got further behind us, the crowds of people thinned until we drove through the Yukon Territory, where people seemed to disappear altogether. I felt small and far from home after driving for hours at top speed without encountering a single human. We filled our tank at each gas station regardless of the steep prices. We were aware that there wouldn't be another gas station until one was desperately needed.

As we crossed the Alaska state line, we felt wild and adventurous.

Because we were saving what little money we had, we decided not to stay in hotels. When both of us were too tired to drive, we pulled the truck into a secluded spot and slept until the cold woke us up. Then we would blast the heater and drive further down the road until we were warm enough to sleep again. It wasn't comfortable, but it was affordable.

"Sharla! Wake up!"

I felt my shoulder being rocked back and forth, but I resisted the command to wake up.

"Sharla! You've got to see this!"

"What?" I asked as I pried myself out of my yoga position on the floor of the truck and lifted my head from the accordion folds at the base of the stick shift that I had been using as a pillow.

"You've got to see this. Look in the road."

I rubbed my blurry eyes, and focused on the spot Mike was pointing to. It took a moment for my eyes to adjust, but then I saw it.

"*Canis lupis*," I whispered. A wolf. It was dark, so I couldn't be sure, but I guessed he was gray and black with startling eyes that appeared gold in the moonlight. He sat proudly, king of the road, and slowly scanned his surroundings in a deceivingly lazy motion. Other than the occasional twitch of his pointed ear as he took note of something beyond me, he stood so still he almost blended seamlessly into the black night. The barely discernible sway of his head and his majestic poise were hypnotic, and we both watched in silence.

"The arctic wolf will usually only attack humans when rabid," I said quietly. Then, for a reason I couldn't comprehend, the mighty wolf lifted his nose and howled into the night. Shivers ran down my spine.

"I heard him howl like that earlier," Mike told me. "That's what woke me up, but you slept right through it."

"Look!" I pointed out Mike's window at the distant ridgeline. There, so black it could have just been a trick of the eye, was the outline of a second wolf.

"Another one?" Mike asked. Then, suddenly, the air became electrified with the remote howl. We watched the black form leap and disappear on the hillside.

"They usually travel with their mate and offspring," I stated.

"I think it's time we leave this family alone," Mike decided. "I was getting cold anyway."

I thought the wolf would start and run off at the sound of the engine, but he just watched us leave as if that had been his desire all along.

Alaska amazed us. We climbed an iceberg, snow shoed in the mountains, and flew in a small plane around the top of Mount McKinley. We gasped in awe at the brilliant turquoise water set against the black sand beach. We pitched a tent where the tide had gone out and woke up to puddles that had frozen to ice during the night. We went to get ice cream one sunny evening and had to turn around when we realized it was nearly midnight. We had never seen a place more beautiful or more full of adventure.

"We've been here for the entire month of May, but it only seems like a few days," Mike said after a late evening walk in the bright sunshine. We couldn't get used to the sun shining for most of the day.

"Alaska has been everything I hoped it would be."

"But, it isn't the place for us, is it?" Mike asked softly.

"No. It's not," I concurred.

"I've been feeling the need to get going," Mike said sadly.

"I have, too," I admitted. "I love it here so much, and I want to stay longer. But, I feel the need to get going, too."

So, after a month in Alaska, we headed back to Iowa and our jobs at the marina.

We had experienced Alaska, and we drove back home on a cloud of adventure and young love.

BABY TIME

After we returned from Alaska, Mike finished his last semester of college, and was offered a job as a youth pastor to about seven faithful teenagers at a small church in Cedar Falls, Iowa. He made $150 a week with no raises. For that reason, he procured a second job at a software store at the mall, and he also built and sold computers. I had interrupted progress toward my degree from the University of Northern Iowa when we were married, so now that we were back where we started, I enrolled in school again.

Our life became a chaotic swirl of chemistry labs, computer assembly, studying, and all-night youth events. Connecting with the teenagers on Wednesday nights was our favorite activity. The group was growing, and we became quite close to the teenagers who regularly showed up. It was a great group of students, and we felt honored to be a part of their lives.

We had been married three years when I spotted a wrapped birthday gift hidden beneath my pillow. Mike was a brilliant gift-giver and understood that my birthday was one of my favorite days of the year, so I knew it would be good. I was turning twenty-three, and, so far, life was adventurous and exciting.

Then, suddenly, my soul felt parched.

In my mind I saw chubby legs, tiny toes, fuzzy hair. I saw round eyes as blue as the inside of a flame twinkling above red, chubby cheeks. I was terrified of the responsibility of having children, but I was utterly aware of their absence. I felt them inside of me just as surely as I could feel the beat of my own heart. Their potential lingered there just awaiting life. Emptiness consumed me - as powerful as a black hole. I reached my hand to my abdomen but hovered just above the skin, afraid the hollowness would swallow up any living flesh. I glowered at the flat stomach that mocked me. It made me feel one-dimensional and selfish.

I ran to the bathroom and threw away the items we used to prevent pregnancy. I briefly wondered if I should check with Mike first, but I recalled that he had once expressed a desire for ten children, and I decided he would not object. I resisted being a mother until I reveled in it, like waking up on a Saturday.

After a year of being surprised every month to discover that I was not pregnant, we consulted my doctor and discovered that my uterus was tipped at an odd angle. He told us not to give up hope, but becoming pregnant would be difficult. After that we had several very serious discussions about a future without children.

When I was twenty-four, I was consumed with studying for finals while also volunteering my time at our church, and I noticed that I felt extremely sick every evening. I had heard of morning sickness, but I was getting sick at night, so I assumed I had the flu. When finals were over and the first week of June had passed and I still had the flu, I scheduled an appointment with my doctor. I asked Mike to pick me up from my appointment although I hadn't told him I was going in for a pregnancy test; I didn't want either of us to get our hopes up only to be disappointed again.

When he pulled up, I climbed into the small red car we had bought for a fraction of its value at an auction and took a deep breath.

"I probably should have talked to you about this first," I said as he drove toward our small apartment.

"Um, that sounds scary," Mike said.

"It's just that I need to tell you something, and it's a pretty big deal."

"Are you sick?" Mike asked, worried.

"No."

"Just tell me. You're scaring me to death."

"I'm pregnant."

"Pregnant? A baby!"

I nodded and Mike stopped the car on the side of the road.

"We are having a baby?"

"Yes."

"Tell me everything."

"It's really happening," I smiled. "I hope you are happy about this."

"Happy?" Mike asked. "Happy is too little of a word. I'm thrilled. Excited. Delighted."

"Really?"

"I couldn't be more happy. We are having a baby." Then he rolled down the window and shouted, "I'm a dad!" A couple of teenage kids with their hands in each other's back pockets stared at him and crossed to the other side of the street, and a woman pushing a stroller down the sidewalk smiled. "I'm a dad!" he shouted again and again all the way home.

MAKENNA

In 1996, five years after we were married, we had our first child. She had a red, splotchy face and a cone-shaped head. She was perfect. I had no idea what to do with her.

From the first, it was frightening. She was born three days after her due date. My water broke just as I was getting into bed, as fate would have it. Having your water break sounds simple, but it is really quite confusing, especially if you happen to be very tired and about to get into bed. It seems like it should be pretty straightforward, like in the movies - gushing out and leaving a puddle at your feet. In reality, I only experienced a trickle down my leg toward my ankle. No puddle. All I did was giggle and rush to the bathroom wondering if I had had an embarrassing accident. But when I tried climbing back into bed, it happened again—a warm trickle down my leg. Without waking Mike, I called my doctor, who I was sure would tell me I was overreacting and not to worry. He told me to get to the hospital.

But getting to the hospital was not easy. First of all, waking Mike requires the use of drums, a foghorn, or any other loud, obnoxious device. Once he was semiconscious, I informed him that my water had broken and we needed to leave. That snapped him into alertness, and we quickly gathered items we would later discover were totally unnecessary, like cards, books, and clothes I had no hope of wearing out of the hospital since they looked like I had last worn them when I was twelve.

Because it was 2:00 AM and we were giddy with nerves only first-time parents can relate to, the hospital was not where we remembered, and in our rush, we became hopelessly lost. I have no idea what happened after that because pain, the likes of which cannot be described with mere words on paper, gripped my abdomen.

Eighteen hours later, a tiny baby girl entered the world by means of an emergency C-section. We named her Makenna Danae. She was tiny and sick, and tubes were inserted into her body at various places. She was helpless and too little to be poked with so many needles. The doctors and nurses prodded at her until she cried, and I wanted to scream at them to get away from her. They took blood from her tiny heel and left a scab that seemed out of place on such a silky surface.

She had beta strep. She had stubbornly remained inside me too long without the bubble of water surrounding her, protecting her. She was exposed and infected by bacteria living inside of me.

The nurses whispered and looked at me with pity in their eyes. They warned me that this soft baby was in great danger. They told me that a baby had died of the same illness just the week before, and when they thought I wasn't looking, they felt Makenna's weak body and shook their heads.

I wanted to shout at them that they were wrong. I knew this child better than anyone else did. She was the one who had kept me awake endless nights with her persistent kicking. She had kept me from eating any fruit for nine long months. She had taken over my body until I hardly recognized myself. She was not as weak as she looked.

I meant to tell them that she would surprise them all. I had it on the tip of my tongue to yell at them that they were underestimating her. I was so tired with the birthing of her, though, that sleep engulfed me while the words were still trapped inside my parched and chapped lips.

For seven days I floated in and out of fevered dreams. I dreamed that the tubes pumping antibiotics into Makenna's body turned into snakes and the nurses shook their heads in unison as they watched the snakes slither across her body. I would wake up in my hospital bed, shivering and terrified. Too weak to scream, I would pant until Mike woke and came to my side.

"You're very sick," he whispered as if his loud, strong voice would shatter me. "You're both very sick." His face shocked me; his cheeks were so sunken and pale he barely looked like my husband. His blue eyes were rimmed with red, either from tears or sleeplessness. Or both. He spooned lime Jello into my mouth, and I ate all I could only for the coolness of it.

On the seventh day I woke to colors and solid ground. I opened my eyes and immediately prayed a thankful prayer. The chairs sat firmly upon the ground instead of blending into the walls and floating around, as they had seemed to do on the previous days. The voices made words that I could understand instead of the warped sounds I had experienced in my fevered condition. The sky was blue, the bed white; the flowers next to my head were pink. Nothing was the tainted yellow I had been seeing.

Mike helped me out of bed and held my elbow as my wobbly legs carried me to the neonatal intensive care unit. I saw my baby, tiny and diapered, in her incubator. Her head was bald, and if I hadn't have known already, I couldn't have guessed if she was a boy or a girl. But I did know. I knew her completely. She was part of me—the best part of me.

"She is not improving as quickly as we would like," the doctor told me as we looked at her together. "She is very sick, and I know you are feeling better, but I don't want you to get your hopes up. Your baby still needs a lot of medical attention."

Makenna turned her tiny head, as if she heard the doctor and understood his words. Her mouth made a perfect circle, amused at her own private joke, and that is when I knew. This girl was doing things her own way. She was stronger than anyone suspected. She was going to be fine. We were going to be just fine.

We left the hospital the next day, the doctors shocked at her sudden improvement.

She was precious, and I had never loved anyone more. She made funny faces and cute noises and filled our small apartment with soft blankets and sweet-smelling lotions. She slept during the day and cried at night. She laughed for no reason and cried for no reason. She was fragile and totally dependent and a complete mystery. I was terrified constantly.

JOSIAH

When Makenna was three months old, I took her to her checkup and mentioned to the pediatrician that my C-section was healing poorly. I was dog-tired and a bit nauseous. He suggested I take a pregnancy test on the spot to rule out that particular explanation before he sent me to my regular doctor.

When he reentered the room, he looked a little frightened and asked me to sit down and remain calm. To my utter astonishment, he announced that a second little one was on the way and had the exact same due date as Makenna's, February 4. When I didn't respond he grew slightly worried and asked a nurse to bring in some water. I came around in a few moments and began laughing. Maybe a little hysterically. The doctor checked my vitals and made me assure him about twenty times that I would be fine. Once I could speak in full sentences again, the doctor allowed me to leave his office.

When I told Mike, his mouth fell open and he didn't speak for several moments. I sat silently, just waiting for my words to make sense to him.

"How did this happen?" he whispered, face blank.

"Probably in the usual way."

"But, we were careful." He swiped his face with his thick hand. "I feel betrayed by science." I saw in his eyes the haunting memories of eight terrifying days in the hospital, days when he thought he would lose one or both of us. Since we had returned from the hospital, he had not been able to settle down. He touched me often, his warm hand on my back or just an elbow bumping against me, as if to assure himself that I was still there. He hadn't slept more than half an hour at a time, constantly running into Makenna's room to check her breathing. He was calmer when she was crying because then he was sure she was okay. I had found him sleeping with her whimpering on his chest. His face was radiant, and he smiled even in his sleep, her baby whine a sweet and reassuring lullaby in his ears.

"It won't be the same as last time," I told him. "I have to talk to my doctor about the details, but the pediatrician told me that they can give me antibiotics before I go into labor so the baby won't be born sick. Even if I am in labor for a long time, the antibiotics would already be in the baby's system. It will be better this time."

"I want to go with you to that appointment just to hear the plan for myself," he said, breathing to drain away his tension. "Another baby?"

"Another baby!"

And then he laughed. Maybe a little hysterically.

When Makenna was five months old, Mike was offered a job as a youth pastor in Omaha, Nebraska. Although we loved our church, the job in Omaha offered us a real salary, which we badly needed with a second baby on the way. I only had one class to complete, and my professor offered to help me finish it through the mail. The best part about moving was our beautiful new apartment with two spacious bedrooms and a dishwasher. I thought our previous unit in married student housing could have fit inside half of our new rental, and I was thrilled that the washer and dryer were right off the kitchen. Just before we moved I had gathered the laundry into a basket and balanced it on the handles of Makenna's stroller as I wheeled it to the Laundromat two blocks from unit 67, where we lived. Now I would just walk to the kitchen to do the laundry, maybe even do it while Makenna napped. I could barely believe how easy my life had become with that one move.

When the baby was seven days past the due date, the doctor declared it was time for the baby to be born whether he or she intended to be or not, so I was given a drug to begin labor. I had been taking antibiotics, but I was given more through an IV. The contractions came in earnest, and I lost all sense of time. I noticed little besides the beeping of the fetal monitor and the blinding pain that consumed me every few seconds. After eleven hours of labor, the monitor beeping out the baby's heartbeat emitted one terrifying, constant beep. Every eye in the room swung to glare at the green dot moving horizontally across the screen without any hope. That single straight line pierced us with terror.

"Everyone besides the father should leave," a nurse said, quickly taking control. She examined the equipment and then felt inside me. "I can feel the baby's head," she said, and the green dot bounced on the screen. I don't know if they taught her this particular skill in nursing school or if she just followed her instinct, but when she rubbed the baby's head, the heart thumped back into action. The rhythmic pulse brought tears to my eyes. I looked at Mike and saw alarm and worry all over him.

The tiny heart pulsed steadily for a half hour before it stopped again. I shut my eyes, fearing to look at Mike. I couldn't let him see my despair, and I couldn't face his horror. I squeezed my eyes shut even when the nurse came and searched again for the baby's head. I continued to keep my eyes closed until the thump of a fragile heart filled the room, and then I lassoed it with my soul and fiercely willed it into my baby. I clung to it with my mind and in my heart. Not caring who heard, I prayed out loud, "I hear and feel this child's heartbeat. God, Please! Make that beat strong!"

Mike grabbed my hand and squeezed, and I felt the steadiness of him seep into me.

"Okay, dear," the doctor said, sweeping into the room like a confident breeze. "You are squeezing your baby too tightly. You should be having short, intense contractions with minutes, or half minutes, between them. However, you have had one long contraction for the past hour. That squeezes the baby's head and doesn't give him a chance to recover. I know you wanted to try to do this the regular way, but I think that plan is over. I suggest an immediate C-section."

"Do it!" I shouted, and Mike nodded his consent.

As the medicine to stop contractions reacted with the medicine to begin contractions, I shook violently. A nurse used soft, warm sheets to secure my arms against the operating table so the shaking wouldn't interfere with the surgery. It took seemingly forever for them to slice me open. I tried to steady my breathing, and I prayed silently inside my head, not wanting to distract the doctor.

"Look at the size of that hand!" the doctor said after an eternity had passed. "This is going to be a big baby!"

"Well," I mumbled, "now I really hope it's a boy."

And he was. He was born with a scowl on his scrunched face, angry at being disturbed. His hands looked enormous on his twig arms, and his huge ears made him look more like an old man than a baby. His howl filled the room and my heart. He wailed and cried as they stitched me back up, and I smiled just listening to his strong lungs pump out their noise. When they finally laid him on my chest, he quieted down.

"I can feel him," I said to Mike who stood by my side silently wiping thankful tears from his cheeks. "I can feel his heartbeat, against my chest. It's strong."

"He is perfect," Mike whispered and then sat and cried into his hands, letting all that fear out. When he could stand up again, he took the stocking hat off the baby's head and studied him.

"He looks mad." I laughed.

"He's not mad. He's determined," Mike said. "Let's name him Josiah."

"That's a good name for him. Josiah Michael." I fell asleep with Mike's touch on my shoulder and Josiah's pounding heart beating against my chest.

DRAKE

When Josiah was three months old, Mike brought a pizza home from work and the smell of it sent me running to the nearest bathroom.

"What's wrong?" Mike asked from the bathroom doorway, forehead creased. "Do you have the flu?"

"There is only one reason I would feel this way right now, and it's not the flu." I moaned, sliding prostrate onto the tile floor.

"What is it? Do you need to go to the doctor?"

"Oh," I whispered, wiping sweat from my forehead, "I'll schedule an appointment eventually. I'm pretty sure I know what I need to do by this point."

"What do you need?" Mike kneeled and helped me to sit with my back against the cool bathtub.

"Prenatal vitamins, saltines, and Sprite." Usually a wordy fellow, Mike sat speechless, eyes vacant, which concerned me. "Mike, I need you to say something."

"I just can't believe it," he said, rubbing his face with his hand. Slowly, he sat next to me, shoulder to shoulder, the two of us leaning against the bathtub as if that was the only thing solid enough to hold us up. "Three babies under the age of two? How will we live through it?"

"Probably with a lot of complaining and hardly any sleeping."

"With all of the advances in modern medicine, you'd think this kind of thing wouldn't happen, and especially not twice. We were careful. We even doubled up on birth control, like the doctor said."

"I know." I held onto his hand, lacing our fingers together, marveling at how tiny my hand was in his and drawing strength from the thickness of his fingers. "I'm sorry."

"No." He shook his head. "No, don't be sorry. I'm not sorry. I'm surprised—shocked, in fact. But I'm not sorry we created a baby together. This baby, whether it is a boy or a girl, must be pretty special if it can overcome the obstacles it had to go through just to be created."

I thought about that. Having a baby wasn't the next thing on my to-do list, and, honestly, I hadn't quite recovered from the prior two C-sections. However, a life had broken through two forms of birth control and was growing inside of me. A little baby, no longer than a grain of rice, had already made itself known.

"I guess if a little baby can do such amazing things, like get created as well as cause me to not want any pizza, it must be a pretty powerful person." I smiled at Mike and squeezed his hand. "Actually, I'm kind of excited to meet such a person."

We soon owned everything in triplicate: three car seats, three cribs, three kinds of pacifiers. We decided to have a planned C-section and skip over the exhausting labor that never seemed to actually birth a baby from me. Another son, Drake Andrew, was born and was perfect. Since he had never experienced the contractions of labor, he had a beautifully shaped head.

The doctor placed him in my arms, and I gazed in wonder at his porcelain skin. He sucked at nothing and made baby noises as he slept. I watched every movement and wondered what kind of person could actually force his way into existence. He smiled in his sleep, and I knew life with him would be an adventure.

Nine days after his birth, our oldest baby turned two. Four days after that, our second baby turned one. We took shifts sleeping and considered ourselves wildly successful if we talked in coherent sentences.

YET ANOTHER BABY

I hadn't had time to make any friends in our new city, and Mike took our only car to work every day, so I was friendless and car-less. I remember thinking that being alone with babies day after day was a stringent test of one's sanity.

But, just before Drake was born, we had moved from our apartment to a house, and the best thing in the world happened: the next-door neighbor, Shelly, became my best friend. I rediscovered adult language. I changed out of my pajamas and started brushing my teeth before noon.

We ripped out the fence that separated our backyards, and Shelly and I spent our days talking while our kids played together. Drake was a newborn, Josiah was one, and Makenna was two, and Shelly had just had her first baby, Brett. The two of us would meet outside after breakfast and let our kids play in the sand and crawl in the grass.

When winter came, we moved our preschool activity back and forth between our two living rooms. Shelly had another baby boy and named him Jake, so there were two moms and five children. Sometimes one of us would watch all the kids while the other one would drive to the gas station and purchase icy-cold fountain drinks. We would sip our drinks and talk and keep each other sane.

We both rejoiced as warm weather rolled back into town and we relocated to the backyard. Makenna was three and discovered how to flood the backyard with water from the hose while the boys covered each other with mud and sidewalk chalk. Shelly and I talked like adults while the children wore themselves out in the sunshine.

"Mike wants to have a fourth baby," I told her one blazing afternoon.

"Really?" she asked, pulling some grass out of her son's mouth. "Do you want to have another baby?"

"I just can't stand the thought of being pregnant again. I always get so sick. And these three keep us so busy, I really don't know how we could possibly manage another," I said, pointing to the large patch of bare ground where the kids were using the hose to make a mud swamp. "We agreed to think about it for a month and then talk about it again."

My days were so full of diaper changing, baths, ear infections, and coloring books that I had very little time to actually consider having another baby. Just the thought of it froze the breath inside my throat. Three years earlier I didn't have any children. I had three now, and I felt like I was drowning under the weight of them.

Two things happened, though, during that month that came out of nowhere and left me astounded.

"Hello!" said a cheerful voice over the phone. "My name is Kim, and I go to your church."

"Hi," I said.

"This is going to sound strange," she said, laughing, "but I have three kids that I homeschool. They are home all day, and I would like to teach them about serving people in need. With all those babies, I bet you could use some help. I wonder if you would let us come over once a week and clean your house for you."

"You would clean my house?" I asked, blinking back tears.

"From top to bottom, once a week, for free!"

I didn't know how she would take it if I had a complete meltdown, so I pushed down my emotions of overwhelming gratitude and agreed. When they arrived at my front door, I noticed three brown-headed children smiling behind their mom. "You have three children, too?"

"Yes," she nodded, and then her smile faltered. "But we should have had four," she whispered, and I wondered if she knew I could still hear her. "Sometimes I look around the table as we eat supper and I get the feeling that we have one empty space."

I gasped as I thought about our table and how there was always one empty chair. She seemed startled, but regained her smile quickly as she gathered her three kids and breezed into my house with her vacuum. I walked as though I were in a trance to the table and stared at the extra chair. I could picture Mike and I, at the ends, and the three kids laughing and eating, but that space glared at me.

I talked to her about it years later, and she doesn't remember saying that. But I will never forget it.

The second thing happened after church one Sunday. I stopped at a table in the lobby to look at some books that were for sale. I wasn't actually interested in buying one; I was just waiting for Mike to finish a conversation so we could go home.

"Do you read a lot?" asked an elderly man from the other side of the table.

"Oh, not really," I said as I quickly put the book down.

"Busy with kids, huh?" he laughed, pointing to Drake who was climbing me as if I were a tree.

"Yeah, I have three." I heaved Drake onto my back and grabbed Josiah's hand before he knocked over a book display.

"My wife and I have three kids, too." The man smiled. "I'll tell you something, though." He leaned toward me and beckoned me closer. "We should have had four."

"What?" I gasped, heart thumping.

"I was tired, and I was scared. I didn't have a great job, and I didn't know how I could provide for three kids, let alone four. But now I know better. I know that there is no fatigue too great to keep a parent from loving another child. And there is nothing better a parent could provide a child with than life—a chance to *be*." He sighed, and his kind eyes echoed with loss. "I love all my kids, but even all these years later, I still feel the emptiness of the fourth child who never was."

EMERY

Emery Morgynn, our fourth child, was born nine months later, in May of 2000. She made our family perfect—two boys and two girls. She filled our hearts and completed us.

We brought her home two days after her scheduled C-section to a two-year-old Drake, a three-year-old Josiah, and a four-year-old Makenna. As he had every time we brought a baby home, Mike set the table with our fine china and placed an old overstuffed recliner near the kitchen so I could sit and rock the baby as he cooked the meal I requested—grilled cheese and crab legs. It was the only time that combination sounded good to me, and I still can't explain why it did.

After Mike cleaned up the kitchen and I fed Emery, we all stood in a circle around her and watched her as she slept on a blanket on the floor. She looked too tiny for all the love we had for her. I looked at the faces of my children, who gazed at her in wonder and awe, and I knew that we were full.

MIKE'S JOURNAL
9/15/2000

W hat if. Dangerous words.

I have my own *what if.* What if sin happens in heaven? The Bible never tells us clearly that sin is absent in heaven. In fact, we are clearly informed that the sin of pride took place in heaven when the angel Lucifer grew prideful in his heart. His sin ultimately led to him getting kicked out of heaven along with a third of the angels who sided with him.

This terrifies me. What if I make it all the way through this life and enter heaven, only to fall to sin there and get kicked out? While I believe, because it is what I have been taught, that sin is not possible in the next life because we have been perfected, what if it is? And, more horrifying, what if I am its victim?

This slim possibility motivates me to eradicate sin, great and small alike, from my heart. I am motivated to not only overcome, but to eradicate, temptation.

With this logic in mind, I prayed a prayer tonight that Sharla felt was dangerous. I asked the Lord to bring to light any hidden sin that I am presently unaware of, and by whatever means necessary, strip it from my heart. Sharla fears that my prayer signed us up for an over-whelming battle. I, however, feel that any mortification in this life that would ensure in me a pure heart is worth the necessary process.

Sharla prays for mercy, but I pray for totality.

SLEEPY WATER

I didn't know it when I married him, but Mike is a gifted story-teller. He tells stories the way a gaffer spins glass. Each night he would gather the kids in a circle on the bedroom floor and tell a small part of an elaborate story. The four main characters in the stories were always our four kids. Sometimes they would have magical powers and go on elaborate adventures with elves. Sometimes they were pirates hunting for treasure at far ends of the earth. He made it up as he told it, and the kids were enthralled.

One time the characters in the story were given a riddle to solve before the next part of the story could be told. The children relentlessly harangued me for two solid days for clues to the answer to the riddle. When they finally solved the riddle and the story could continue, I was as relieved as they were.

But Mike often had to travel out of town, and then I was on bedtime duty by myself. After attempting several times to enthrall the kids with my clever stories like their dad could do, I got the message loud and clear that my stories were hopelessly boring. So I resorted to reading book after book until at least one set of eyes drooped shut. Usually mine.

One of the glorious things about having four children four years old and under is that they all go to bed by eight o'clock. The problem is that when one child has a hard time falling asleep the three others copy the behavior until you want to chew nails and then spit them at somebody.

With so many children going to bed at the same time, we weren't big believers in post bedtime activity. It was like dominos—once one child needed a drink, they all lined up to receive the suddenly needed drink. It could go on and on for hours. Drinks, blankets, and imaginary friends all had to wait until morning.

Makenna was the worst at engaging in delaying tactics. There was no end to the emergencies she could invent once the sun went down. She was sweaty, she was freezing, her eyes wouldn't stay shut, she forgot how to fall asleep, her arms stopped bending; she could go on forever.

One evening was particularly bad. Mike had been out of town for over a week, and I hadn't left the house for that entire time. Makenna stayed in her bed the same amount of time she would have if it had been on fire, which inspired the other three to join our party in the kitchen. At one point I stood at the sink handing forbidden drinks to four bright-eyed children an hour past bedtime and wondered if sleeping in a pile on the kitchen floor might be more successful than having them actually fall asleep in their soft, warm beds.

I finally managed to get everybody back in bed, tucked in again, and the house was quiet. I thought that they had finally settled in for the night when I heard the all-too-familiar footsteps in the hallway. I knew it was Makenna without even looking. It was always Makenna. Complete exhaustion enveloped me like a hot, humid cloud, and tears filled my eyes. I felt so frustrated that my hands actually shook.

"What is it now, Makenna?" I asked without looking at her, drying my tears.

"I tried really hard, Mommy, but my eyes won't stay shut. They just pop back open so I can't sleep. Can't you give me something for it?"

I took a few deep breaths and teetered on the brink of losing my patience. In the space of one heartbeat, I concocted a plan. I plastered a very serious expression on my face and turned to her.

"Yes," I told her. "I can give you something, but it is very strong. It might be too strong for such a little girl."

"What is it?"

"It is called sleepy water, and it is a magic potion that I learned in chemistry class."

"I want some," she sang, dancing around the kitchen.

"I shouldn't give it to you because it will make you fall asleep almost instantly, and you will sleep so hard you won't be able to leave your bed until breakfast time."

"I want some." She danced.

After some very serious consideration, I told her, "All right. I will make some for you. But you have to promise me something."

"I will."

"After you drink it, you have to run—not walk—to your room and lay in your bed. You can't get out of your bed for any reason except a real emergency. This stuff is so powerful you might fall asleep right on the floor if you don't get in bed soon enough. Can you do that?"

She nodded solemnly "I will do it, Mommy. I promise."

I made a big production out of filling a small cup with water and adding a squirt of lemon juice. I stirred it with a straw ten times in a clockwise direction. Then I carefully added three granules of sugar and stirred twice in a counterclockwise direction.

"Remember," I warned, as I handed the cup to my wide-eyed troublemaker, "drink this quickly and then run straight to your bed and stay there."

"Okay," she whispered in awe as she stared at her magic potion. She raised the cup to her lips and swallowed it all in two gulps. She didn't even take the time to place the cup on the counter but just threw it in my direction as she scurried to her room. Five minutes later she was sound asleep.

We didn't resort to sleepy water every night but reserved it for those ultra vexing situations in which someone tried and tried but just couldn't remember how to fall asleep. But when we needed it, it was there for us. It always worked like magic.

MOVING

Just before Makenna started kindergarten, our home church from Des Moines called to ask if Mike would be interested in the youth pastor position. We had settled into Omaha and had no desire to move. However, the more we thought about it, the more we realized how much we would love to raise our kids in closer proximity to their cousins and grandparents. I was barely holding onto my sanity raising the kids with Mike so busy working, and I knew that being in the same city as my mom was an unparalleled opportunity.

The church in Des Moines was more conservative than the church we were used to in Omaha, and it was smaller, but since it was our home church, we had a soft spot in our hearts for it. We decided to take the job, so, in August of 2001, we moved. To this day, one of the hardest things I have ever done is wave good-bye to Shelly and drive out of town.

We bought a house previously occupied by four college guys, so there was quite a bit of work that needed to be done before the house was livable, but it had a lot of potential and a pool in the backyard. We finished the kids' rooms first, and Mike and I slept on a mattress on the dining-room floor while we built a bedroom for ourselves.

We soon discovered that the staff of our new church had some rules that surprised us. For example, the pastors were not allowed to see a movie in a movie theater, and wearing jeans to church was frowned upon. And when we needed help, we didn't know exactly what to do about it. The pastors in Omaha had always made a point of praying for each other's families and offering understanding and help when families struggled. However, this church was very different. We, Mike especially, felt an unspoken pressure to make sure we fit the expectations of what the staff wanted us to be. Instead of asking for help, we began trying to keep our struggles quiet and private.

There were moments we wondered what we had gotten ourselves into, but, after two years of hard work, we formed a group of adult youth leaders, and those people became valued friends to us. We dearly loved them and cherished their friendship.

I know now that the environment we grew used to there was not a healthy one for us. It is never a healthy lifestyle when your struggles are seen as unacceptable. When you cannot ask for help because you are afraid to let anyone see your imperfections, you are headed down a dangerous path. Our love for our youth leaders, the closeness of family, and the consuming responsibility of safely delivering four children to their beds at the end of each demanding day blinded us to the peril we were racing toward.

MIKE'S JOURNAL
6/1/2002

I have a surprise for Sharla. It has been awhile since the two of us have really connected. We try to talk after we put the kids to bed, but she usually falls asleep. I try to remind myself that she's exhausted from taking care of the kids, but I admit it feels like she is uninterested in me when she falls asleep while I am talking.

I've been making a consistent effort to help with the kids the instant I walk in the door. It's not hard—I love their slobbery, happy greetings. I know Sharla needs a break, so I have been doing what I can. I'm tired after work, but she is, too. I now do the dishes after supper so she doesn't have to worry about it. I also pick up their toys during bath time so the house is clean at the end of the day. Another thing I love to do is tell the kids long stories at bedtime. I hoped this would give Sharla a chance to relax, but she still seems so tired.

Our kisses have grown few.

I decided to shave my goatee. Sharla says she likes it, but I know it scratches her when we kiss.

NAUGHTY MOUSE

Drake was fascinated by any and all wildlife. He was usually holding a cricket or a moth or something else he had found. At first I told him, "Put that down right now because it is dirty and gross." But, since he never stopped, and since I had four small children, and since I was exhausted, and since it kept him interested in something besides biting his older brother in the back (Josiah still has the scar), I relented and let the child play with the grosser things in life.

Then, one day, he ran to me with his teary cheeks bouncing, and told me, "A mouse bit me!"

"How did you get bitten by a mouse?" I asked as I examined his red and swollen thumb.

"I was holding it, and it bit me," he cried.

"How did you hold a mouse?"

"It was on the ground, and I saw it, and I caught it."

"Didn't the mouse run away from you when you tried to catch it?" I know that field mice can run up to fifteen miles per hour.

"It was running, and I was faster."

"So the mouse was running away from you, and you chased it down and were able to catch it?" I asked skeptically, looking at his chubby little legs.

"Well, it was running and jumping, and I was faster than that," he said and nodded.

I remembered watching a mouse run around as my uncle chased it with a broom when I was a nanny so many years before. I remembered clearly how terrifying it was to see the mouse dash back and forth but never get caught. So, I knew from experience that mice are terrifying and will haunt your nightmares for years. And they are fast.

For these reasons, I admit that I had a hard time believing that a four-year-old with legs covered in fat folds could actually move fast enough to catch a mouse. But a small voice in the back of my head said to believe this small boy. With my own eyes, I had seen him do stranger things.

"Well," I tried to reassure him, "the mouse was probably scared when you picked it up, so it bit you out of fear."

"No, it wasn't scared when I picked it up. It was nice then. It got scared when I tried to feed it to the cat."

MIKE'S JOURNAL
6/5/2002

I shaved my goatee. Sharla didn't notice.

LOCUST DRAMA

Science, instead of landscaping, was my passion, so the kids were free to dissect flowers, dig for rocks, break sticks, flood the grass with hose water, or do anything else that made sense in the mind of a curious child. I loved spending afternoons in the sunshine and had a hard time enforcing naps on beautiful days. So, even though I knew I would pay for it later, one especially gorgeous day in July, I let them play with sidewalk chalk, splash in the pool, and catch bugs instead of nap. Makenna was six and Josiah was five, so they usually spent naptime playing quietly in their rooms with books and puzzles. However, the entire family was better off if Drake and Emery spent at least an hour sleeping.

I spread a blanket in the shade and placed Emery in the center with a slice of watermelon. She was two, but was still slowly getting teeth, which the dentist assured me was okay after I demanded x-rays at her one-year-old appointment to verify her teeth existed. I knew she would soothe her swollen gums on the cool rind for a long time, so I challenged the other three kids to a game of hide and seek. Their fine blond hair smelled of baby shampoo and toddler sweat and blew in the breeze like the puff off a dandelion. It is etched in my memory, and I replay it like a movie even now.

"Hey, kids!" I called from the shade of an old, fat, tree stump. "Come look at the cicada shell."

Sweaty bodies carried by chubby legs came running as I held the crispy shell in my palm at their eye level.

"People often call this a locust shell, but it is actually the empty skin of a cicada that dug its way out of a deep tunnel in the earth and then molted on this stump. That cicada, wherever it is, is now an adult."

"Can I hold it?" Makenna asked in a whisper, as if her breath might crush the delicate skin. Her fascination, however, quickly turned to horror once the prickly legs touched her fleshy palm. Her tiny screech magnified into an increasingly louder scream and her wide eyes bored into the empty shell as if it might, at any time, contaminate her.

I grabbed the shell away from Makenna and placed it into Josiah's impatiently grabbing hands. His fascinated eyes grew large as he moved his hand around in order to observe the shell from every angle. He held it up to the sunlight and his lips formed a silent *O* when the light illuminated the inside.

Drake was stomping his feet and demanding his turn, so I placed the shell into his hand which immediately clamped down on it and ground it into sand. Josiah wailed and threw himself to the ground in despair, and I figured it was time for a snack.

MIKE'S JOURNAL
10/5/2002

I am sick with defeat. I feel separate. Sharla is like an island. She just carries on, unaffected by wind or tide. The years roll past, and she doesn't need me. It has been longer than I can remember since we had a meaningful conversation. I've done everything I can think of to get her to notice me. I started working out. I help around the house. I rub her shoulders and feet. Every time I try to hold her hand or kiss her I feel like a junior-high boy asking a girl to approve of him. That fear of being rejected doesn't go away once you are married. When I try to talk to her about this, she nods and listens, but her expression tells me she thinks I am making a big deal out of nothing.

I took a class at church called Christ Life hoping to solve myself. It was a great class, but I am still broken.

I took a giant risk and asked the other pastors on staff if we could be accountable and open with each other. I'm not sure who else I can talk to that might understand what is happening to me. I asked them twice. They said no. Actually, they said less than no by ignoring my request completely. Twice. It was as if my voice made no sound.

So, I'm going to ask Sharla to go to marriage counseling with me. We can't afford it, but we can't afford not to. I asked around and made an appointment with someone who is very respected. And expensive.

Please, God, let this work.

BLANKET THEATER

lanket Theater started with a very complicated process of choosing a movie to watch. The kids would place every movie we owned on the living room floor and eliminate them one by one. Whichever movie was left was the one we watched. However, they rarely agreed and debated extensively over which movie should be eliminated.

"I don't want to watch this one," Josiah might say, "because it's a girl movie." This would provoke a lengthy debate from Makenna who loved girl movies. Emery didn't really get a vote because she could not speak clearly enough. Whenever she attempted to say *movie* it came out sounding like *boobie*.

It would have been helpful if I had explained this situation to my dad, who volunteered to babysit one night. Since Emery pronounced the word *watch* to sound like *wash*, she told him, "Gampa, I wanna wash a boobie."

He had no response.

The movie debate could last a very long time but only rarely ended in a full-fledged brawl. I let them work it out among themselves while I made a big bowl of popcorn with M&M's sprinkled on top and filled their spill-proof cups with Kool-Aid. After they finally decided on the movie, we spread a big blanket on the floor in front of the TV and sat on it to watch the movie and eat the popcorn. It was Blanket Theater. We loved it.

"Everyone is finally in bed," I told Mike as I plopped onto the couch next to him after Blanket Theater one evening. "I let them skip their naps today, so I told them to sleep late tomorrow morning."

"What are the chances that will happen?"

"Very slim. But I told them not to turn the TV on before eight. That way maybe at least one of them will sleep late."

"How are you feeling?" I heard Mike ask.

"What? I'm sorry," I said, rubbing my eyes. "I think I started to fall asleep."

"Are you sick?"

"No. I'm just so tired. Thanks for cleaning up the popcorn and blanket," I said as I sat up straight and willed myself into alertness.

"I've been thinking," Mike said as he grabbed my hand and fidgeted with my fingers. "What do you think about going to see a marriage counselor?"

"Do we have a problem?"

"No," Mike answered after hesitating a moment too long. "But it seems hard for us to connect with each other, and I think talking to someone about it might be a good idea."

"You know, I used to believe that being married would be like an eternal sleepover with your favorite person. It's not. It's hard."

"Yeah. It seems like there is only enough time to miscommunicate." Mike squeezed my hand and smiled nervously. He looked so scared I wanted to smooth his hair and tell him not to worry. We were both exhausted. I could not think clearly and kept falling asleep at offensive times. Marrying my soul mate, the only person who could light me on fire with one simple look, did not make this problem any easier for us.

Remembering all the times in the past that I had stated my thoughts too bluntly, I tried to consider his feelings and respond sensitively.

"I don't think we have any more problems than the average couple," I heard myself say and realized it sounded harsh instead of comforting. "If you think it will help to talk to a counselor, then let's do it." I leaned my head on his shoulder to show him that everything between us was fine. In the back of my mind, a nagging voice was screaming at me, so I reviewed our conversation in my mind trying to pinpoint what was alarming me. The warmth of Mike's shoulder, though, enveloped me, my thoughts became muddled, and my eyes slid closed. I told myself to remember to think about it later.

I woke up in a dark room and realized I had been asleep for hours. It took a moment to register that I was in bed. Mike must have carried me from the couch when I fell asleep. I rubbed my eyes as a thought danced around in my brain. There was something I needed to do or remember. Something I might notice if I could just open my eyes long enough. The thought flitted around like a vapor, like a smoke signal blown in the wind. I tried to focus on it, but it evaporated into blackness, and suddenly I was an Indian princess with feathers in my hair cheering on my war-painted brothers who were responding to the smoke signal sent from a distant tribe.

MIKE'S JOURNAL
8/7/2003

After spending $500 on counseling, I finally gave up. We went together, and then I went alone. I told him everything. I told him how separate I feel. I told him I feel unimportant and empty. I told him how hard I try to make myself better and better.

He told me I should do some relaxation exercises. I did them.

I'm still broken.

But now I know that I cannot be fixed.

FIRST DAY OF SCHOOL

"Thanks for taking the day off," I told Mike as we walked Emery home in her stroller.

"I know the first day of school is always hard for you," Mike said.

"I just can't believe Drake is in kindergarten! It seems like he should still be collecting roly-polys in his pockets and feeding mice to cats." I had held back my tears while escorting Makenna, Josiah, and Drake to their new classrooms, but as we walked home I let the tears roll down my cheeks.

"I can't believe we have a kindergartener, a first grader, and a second grader," Mike said. "Sometimes I miss the little toddler stage so much it actually hurts."

"I know," I said, unbuckling Emery from her stroller as Mike held our front door open.

"I wanna play with Drakie," Emery told me, out of breath from navigating the front steps.

"We will go get him just before lunch," I said.

"Okay," Emery said running to the table to finish coloring the picture she had started after breakfast. "He makes mine heart light all the way up."

"Emery is so precious," Mike said quietly to me. "And her eyes twinkle like stars."

"Hey Daddy," Emery turned in her chair and said seriously, "the stars are probably the glitter that was leftover when God got done making me."

"I'm sure you are right," Mike laughed. "And you have amazing hearing."

"Yep," she said before returning to her coloring. Once she picked up her crayons and began focusing on her picture, I knew she would be lost in her own artistic world, oblivious to everything else. Art captivated her, and she would often spend an entire morning drawing, pasting, cutting, or writing with a focus that was impressive.

"I had a weird dream last night," Mike said as he loaded the leftover breakfast dishes into the dishwasher. "I had gone to a foreign country, and I didn't know anyone. I didn't know anything about myself: who I was, where I lived, or even my name. I couldn't understand what anyone said to me, and I didn't recognize anything. I woke up sweating."

I didn't know why, but his words set off an alarm in my head. I knew it was just a dream, but it also seemed important.

"Do you think it means anything?" I asked as I returned the orange juice to the refrigerator.

"I don't usually read too much meaning into dreams," he said, but I noticed that his hands shook as he grabbed the dishcloth and began wiping down the counter.

"Something is wrong, isn't it?" I asked, my stomach turning to hot liquid.

"Why do you say that," he turned and looked at me in surprise.

"I'm not sure," I felt my heart hammering but couldn't understand why I was having such a strong reaction to a dream. "I just feel like the dream is some sort of warning."

"Well, I've felt pretty discouraged lately. I've felt for a long time now that my job is consuming, and I don't feel like anyone has my back. It is such a different atmosphere than the church in Omaha. I felt like I could talk to the other pastors there about anything, but I feel like I'm alone here. I've brought it up a couple times, but I just feel needy when I mention it. Nobody else on staff seems to feel the way I feel.

"And I know you are really busy and tired, but I feel alone here too. I know it's just a season, but it's a long one. I was really hoping to get more answers out of my counseling sessions, and I feel frustrated that nothing was solved."

"Have you talked to anyone about this?"

"I've tried to talk to the other pastors, I've paid a lot of money to talk to counselors, I've prayed endlessly, I've fasted, and I've taken all the classes the church offers. That's why I've been discouraged."

"Maybe it is time to move," I suggested. "We've been here almost two years, and if you still feel like nobody has your back, then we need to find someplace else."

"I'd hate to do that to you and the kids. You are all so happy here."

"We will be happy someplace else too. And why don't I see if my mom can watch the kids tonight so we can spend some time alone? We could go eat someplace nice and come home after the kids are asleep."

"I would love to go on a date," Mike said with a smile.

"Mom," Emery wailed suddenly. "I just threw up on the dog!"

"Oh, no," I moaned as I grabbed Emery and ran to the bathroom with her, barely making it to the toilet before she threw up again.

"No, no! Stop!" I heard Mike shout from the kitchen.

"What's wrong?" I called as I held Emery's hair out of her face and tried to hold my breath.

"The dog shook herself off! There's puke all over the place!"

I wet a soft washcloth with warm water and cleaned Emery's trembling mouth.

"How long have you felt sick, Sweetie?"

"Since I threw up," she whimpered.

"Well, I think you should take a nap," I said, noting her warm forehead. "I'm pretty sure you have a fever."

I carried her to her bed and lay beside her until she fell asleep, mere minutes later. When I returned to the kitchen, Mike was scrubbing the floor with disinfectant.

"So much for our date tonight," I said. "Something like this always seems to happen on the nights we plan to go out. Someone gets sick, or you get an emergency phone call, or we can't afford to go anywhere. I'm sorry."

"It's okay," Mike said.

But it wasn't.

BEST FRIEND

"**M**om! Dad!" Josiah ran into the kitchen and pointed to a red splotch on his arm. "Look what Drake did."

"How did he do that?" Mike asked, rubbing the red spot.

"He pinched me."

Mike turned to look at Drake. "Drake, why did you pinch your brother?"

"Because I am crazy," he answered, eyes huge and serious.

"Is it normal for brothers to antagonize each other like that?" I asked Mike after we had taken care of the pinching problem and shoved the boys into the backyard to play. The day was warm, but the smell of cooler weather was in the air. "My brother and I weren't constantly arguing like those two boys are."

"Yeah," he answered. "My brother and I used to fight like crazy. We only started getting along after he moved out of the house."

"There has to be something we can do to encourage them to be friends."

Mike thought about it. "Well, they're pretty different from each other; they do things differently, think differently. They are opposites in a lot of ways, and it doesn't help that they are only eleven months apart in age. They are six and seven now, and their differences are getting more irritating to them. There is a lot of competition between them."

Sharing a room was a major source of stress between them: Drake wanted the room tidy, but Josiah tended to bless the entire room with a covering of his belongings. Josiah, stockier than his brother, won every wrestling match, leaving Drake feeling small and frustrated. Sometimes they just liked irritating each other on purpose. I knew we had a problem at supper one evening. Our custom was to go around the table, everybody taking a turn saying their high and low of the day.

"Makenna," I said spooning lasagna onto her plate, "what was your high and low today?"

"My high was playing with my friends, and my low was when I spilled my pudding at lunch." She smiled, proud of herself for answering the question so brilliantly.

"Emery, what was your high and low?" I continued around the table.

"High was Mommy and Daddy. Low was nap cuz I hate nap." Everyone smiled at her improper grammar, and I kissed the top of her head for saying I was her high.

"Josiah, your turn," I continued. "What was your high and low?"

"My high was building a puzzle, and my low was when Drake tore it apart," he answered seriously, looking at his brother out the corner of his narrowed eyes.

"Okay. Drake, what was your high and low?"

"Mine high was when I broke Siah's puzzle, and mine low was when he told everybody."

It made me laugh, but I knew this antagonistic behavior would only get worse as the boys grew older. I needed to intervene, so I came up with a brilliant plan: brainwashing.

A few nights later I was tucking Josiah into bed while Drake was still finishing his bath, so it was a good time to talk privately. "Do you know who your best friend is?" I asked him as I pulled his covers up.

"What does, 'best friend' mean?" He narrowed one eye.

"A best friend is the person you appreciate and love more than anyone else in the world," I explained, pulling the blankets up to his chin and tucking them around his shoulders.

"Oh, I have one of those."

"Well, who is it?" I asked.

"Me," he replied, lifting his feet toward the ceiling and untucking the blankets from the bottom of the mattress.

"You are your own best friend?" I couldn't help laughing.

"Yep," he answered. "And when I grow up I should make a girl clone of myself and marry it."

"Well, I guess I can scratch the 'be confident in yourself' speech. But, buddy, that's not really how a best friend works. A best friend is someone you can talk to and do things with."

"Yeah. Me."

"But, if you had to pick only one person to tell a very important secret to, who would that person be?" I wrestled his feet back down toward the mattress and sat on them.

"I dunno," he answered.

"Well, I do. It's Drake."

"No," he growled as he tried to lift his feet again.

"Actually, Drake really is your best friend."

"I don't think so," he said after scrunching his face in thought and finally lying still. "He's my brother."

"See," I said from the bottom of his bed as I tucked his blankets back in, "that is exactly why he is the perfect best friend. He is always with you. If you are sick, he can still play with you. He goes on every vacation you go on, you talk to him in your bed at night when you are supposed to be asleep, and someday, when you are very old, you will have children, and he will be their uncle. All your other friends will grow up and many of them will move away and have their own families, but Drake is your family. Even if he moves away, you will still be family."

He thought for a moment, then raised his index finger and said, "But he makes me so mad."

"I know. He can do that. But he also makes you laugh, doesn't he? And he likes making mud with you in the backyard."

"He is pretty funny," he admitted.

"Why don't you just think about it for a while," I encouraged him as I kissed his forehead and turned to leave the room.

"Hey, Mom," he called, and I turned back around. "Do you hear that weird noise?"

"No, I don't hear anything," I told him after listening for a few moments.

"I hear something," he said, a little worried.

"I don't hear anything, buddy."

"Well," he said as he pulled his covers up and turned onto his side, "maybe it's a rat scratching his cheek."

MIKE'S JOURNAL
6/10/2004

It has been a long time since I've written—almost a year. Reading through my prior entries was surprising. Nothing has changed. I wanted a deeper connection with Sharla or, at least, a close friend I could be completely honest and accountable to. But I've just accepted that Sharla doesn't need me. It's okay. She's happy.

I try to tell myself that I don't need her either.

But I do.

TOO LATE

"Remember when we talked a long time ago about moving?" Mike asked after the kids were in bed one evening. "Yeah," I stopped folding the shirt in my hands and looked at him.

"Something came up. How do you feel about Oklahoma?"

"Are you serious?" I asked.

"I've had a couple phone calls from a church there, and it might be just what we are looking for."

"You haven't said anything for so long, I just thought moving wasn't really an option anymore."

"I think it is," he said and glanced away from me.

"Is something wrong?" I asked, sensing trouble I couldn't define.

"No, I'm excited about the church that called. It sounds like just what I've been wishing this church was. If it isn't too late, I'd be very interested in working there."

"Too late?" I asked, "Too late for what?"

"What?" Mike asked.

"You said, 'If it isn't too late.' What did you mean by that?"

"I said that?" Mike asked. "I don't know why I said that. I just feel that my prayers might finally be answered. They want us to come visit."

"Have you been looking for job openings?"

"No," Mike answered. "I just kept thinking that if I prayed hard enough, God would provide an answer to my problems here without making you and the kids move. Then I got this phone call, and I just kept thinking that I wish it had happened sooner."

"I wonder what the schools are like in Oklahoma," I said as I resumed folding the mountain of laundry before me.

"At least the kids are in first, second, and third grade - still young enough to change schools without too much trouble."

"Well," I said, "let's go there and see if this place is as good as you think it might be."

As we went to bed that night, I wondered why I felt unsettled. Talking about moving was a good reason, but I had the feeling that there was something I was missing – like I blinked too long and missed something important. I turned off the light and walked the few feet to the bed with my arms stretched, searching in the dark for the soft destination. When I climbed in, Mike put his head on my shoulder and held me so tightly I could barely breathe. I wrapped my arms around his shoulders and wondered what was wrong.

"I miss you so much," Mike said, squeezing me even tighter.

"Miss me?" I asked. "I'm right here." I almost laughed, but I could tell that he was serious.

"You are and you aren't," he said.

I had just opened my mouth to ask what he meant by that when my shoulder was assaulted by the tiniest, so the scariest, of touches, and surviving ghoulish night-dwellers became my only concern. I screamed and grabbed the first thing I could find, which was Mike's ear. I yanked it backward and forward as fight mode took over my instincts. Infected by the sudden panic, Mike roared and kicked his feet so hard that all of the covers sailed across the room. Terrified by the immediate increase in volume, Josiah, who had been the night-dweller to tap me on my shoulder, shouted and pounded his fists into my mattress. A few seconds into the madness, it slowly began to dawn on me that my innocent seven-year-old son had tapped my shoulder, and there was no imminent danger. I stopped trying to rip Mike's ear off his head, and I began to giggle.

"What in the world is going on?" Mike shouted out of the dark.

"It's just Josiah," I explained, turning to see if Josiah was permanently scarred by our terrifying behavior.

"I had a bad dream," Josiah said, voice wobbly.

"Well, I hope that helped," Mike joked, rubbing his ear.

Josiah chuckled and climbed into bed beside me as Mike picked up the covers and spread them over the bed. I kept picturing all three of us screaming at each other in the dark bedroom, and I cracked up so hard I shook the whole bed. Soon we were all laughing loudly, and picturing that made me laugh even harder, and I struggled to breathe. It took several minutes for the adrenaline-fueled hilarity to subside.

"What was your bad dream about, Josiah," Mike asked after we had calmed down.

"Monsters with green eyeballs," Josiah answered in a soft voice.

I put my hand on his forehead and felt his hot skin.

"Here we go," I told Mike. "He's burning up." Josiah rarely got sick, but, when he did, he spent the course of the night passing from one terrible nightmare into another. The doctor had told us that he would probably outgrow his night terrors, but it was harrowing when it happened. He had fallen back to sleep and was already twitching and mumbling about monsters with stretchy hands.

I never knew what would calm him down. It usually got a lot worse if I tried to wake him up, and he was so big it was difficult for me to hold him. I knew I would resort to the only thing I could do – pray and sing songs he knew and liked. It didn't make his nightmares go away, but it usually kept him from growing hysterical. It meant a long sleepless night, and I knew Mike had to get up early in the morning for work.

"I'll take him to his bed and stay with him tonight," I told Mike. "You need your sleep, and I can nap when Emery naps tomorrow."

"I miss you," I heard him say as I guided Josiah out of our bedroom.

BAD DELIVERY OF BAD NEWS

"Remember Sarah Copeland from my elementary school?" I asked my mom over the phone as I shook my finger at Drake and Josiah who were using the time I was distracted to pick a fight with each other. Josiah was making faces at Drake, and Drake was shoving Josiah's favorite Hot Wheels car in his underwear.

"Yes," Mom answered as Drake shook his booty toward Josiah, Hot Wheels obviously protruding from his underwear.

"She is dead," I told her.

"What?" Mom screamed, bursting into tears.

"She was in a car accident," I explained as Josiah finally lost patience and tackled Drake to the ground.

"Oh, Sharla! You can't just say it like that," Mom wailed as Drake rubbed the underwear-contaminated car on Josiah's chest.

"How should I say it?" I asked, confused.

"Ease into it more than that."

"Why? How?"

"Just don't say it so shockingly. Her mom is a friend of mine. I'll call you back later." Mom sobbed and hung up the phone as Josiah head-butted Drake in the stomach.

"I need to sign myself up for social school," I said to myself putting the phone down. After a very successful trip to the church in Oklahoma, Mike had accepted the position there, and I had intended on telling my mom that we would soon be moving. However, when she hung up in tears about the way I had told her about the death of my friend, I decided that I should work on my delivery skills before breaking news of our move to her. "Boys, you know what to do."

"Fine," they grumbled as they each stomped into a separate bedroom and shut the door.

We had rules for our children to help them get along with each other. If they were picking on each other, they were to go to separate rooms until they could behave pleasantly. Also, they were not allowed to cheer against a sibling during a game. So, if Josiah and his friend, John, were playing chess, Drake should cheer for Josiah. If he didn't want to, he should remain silent.

Another rule was that they should stick up for each other in public. If they had a problem, they should work it out at home, privately, and not speak poorly about their sibling to their friends. If they saw each other in a public place, like passing each other in the hallway at church or school, they were to at least smile and possibly wave. No ignoring each other.

Over time, they developed a very special friendship, the boys especially. They could almost always communicate without speaking a word and were unstoppable during a game of Pictionary. They talked and laughed in their bedroom at night when they were supposed to be falling asleep, and they often kept the girls awake with their obnoxious behavior.

"Boys!" Mike called to them when they should have been asleep that night, "Be quiet. I want some peace."

"Dad," Emery answered, "you can do peace in my room!"

I smiled and didn't know my happy life was an illusion.

MIKE'S JOURNAL
11/1/2004

Can even God save me from this body of death? I struggle to believe that He can. I can only hope. I deeply beg God to free me. Everything that can be shaken has been shaken, and I am left with nothing. I feel almost nothing. I think shallowly, and I speak foolishly. If I ever needed to be delivered, it is now.

I have brought destruction upon my family, my friends, my kids, my church, and, most painfully, my wife. Now I have to live with the destruction I have wrought. It is uncomfortable knowing all my sin is out for the world to see. My motivation to go forward at this point is only to look into the distant future where I have worked out my salvation.

I have very little hope that my marriage will make it through this. I don't see how my kids will ever have a father they can be proud of. I can't comprehend life ever being fun or happy again.

The price is so great. Why have I been such a fool?

MORNING AFTER

A girl can be all grown up, but when she is really hurting, she wants her mommy and daddy. I don't know how I did it without running my car off the road, but after the sleepless night I spent praying for Mike to die, I drove to my parents' house. Since I got out of bed before dawn, the kids were still sleeping when I left my house, and, since Mike was still alive, I felt that he was more than able to handle morning childcare.

I have no memory of the drive to their house or parking the car, but I remember walking in the front door and falling onto the floor in a wailing heap. Between sobs, I explained the situation to them, and although I expected them to look at each other and concoct a plan sure to remove Mike from this earth, they shocked me by saying things like, "Everything will be okay," "We will help you guys through this," "We will work this out together," and, "We know Mike, and this is out of character." Then they tucked me into their bed with assurances that they would cancel all of their plans and spend the day watching Emery, who was four and not yet in school, and getting the other kids to and home from school.

Some parents are pretty much worthless. Mine are the opposite of that. I don't know how God decided to give me the wisest parents who ever graced the earth, but I am certain that without their guidance, I would be a bitter shell of a woman. From the beginning of this nightmare they spoke words of encouragement and hope to me. I thought they were crazy and naive and optimistic, but I still heard them.

I think those first twenty-four hours were crucial in placing our marriage on a path toward restoration, and my parents were almost single-handedly responsible for the wisdom and grace it took to do so.

I found out later that they drove straight to my house and called Mike into the front yard, knowing the kids would soon begin to wake up, and confronted him there so none of the kids would hear the conversation. He expected them to be carrying knives or throwing socks, but instead, with tears in their eyes, they told him they thought of him as a son and would do whatever it took to help him make his life right. They knew his actions were not in line with his character, and they knew he needed help.

I cannot explain when these two people who raised me were bequeathed with the Wisdom of Solomon because I remember that they were completely ridiculous when I was sixteen. They wouldn't let me call boys on the phone and made sure I was home by ten. They were old-fashioned, outdated, and annoyingly intrusive.

Grace is sometimes sharper than a dagger. I know now that Mike could have accepted an angry shouting tirade, a punch in the jaw, or even a mortal wound, but because of the grace shown to him by the most unexpected of people, he was undone. Although I didn't care at the time, he cried as he begged them to help him.

MIKE'S JOURNAL
11/3/2004

All that I have is gone, and all that I desire has been stripped from me. I have nothing.

I look back and wonder what happened. How could I have done the things that I did? Why was my heart not screaming at me? How did my conscience get so seared? I have thought a lot about causes. What could have caused this? Obviously, I resisted the Holy Spirit's conviction, even when it was the strongest.

Who was I to think I could fool God?

God, I would gladly cling to you, but my strength is gone. I'll lie here and rot unless you pick me up. I know you are teaching me to be selfless, but has it come too late? Am I too far gone? Can you redeem one as wretched as me?

ALONE

One conversation had left my life in ruins. My family was shattered. My church was gone. My friends were gone. I felt like a disease.

Mike lost his job instantly, of course, and was told he could not ever come back to that church. Our salary was cut off immediately, and our health insurance was discontinued. We were told not to contact any of our youth leaders, our only friends. The senior pastor cried with us and gave us gift cards to restaurants, but his footsteps out of our house sounded like the pounding of a gavel.

I knew there would be no help for us from a place where pastors were not allowed to enter a movie theater. I stared hopelessly into the future searching for a way to raise four children with no health benefits, no income, no church, no friends, and a husband I wished was dead.

I was alone.

Of course, the thought of divorce ran through my head every nanosecond, but I had been a stay-at-home mom for eight years, since my first daughter was born, and I had no financial options of my own to fall back on. I was tempted to just pack the kids and go somewhere far away. I knew I could get a job, even if it didn't pay much. But a small voice of reason kept me from making that rash decision. While I would surely find employment, it would likely not pay enough to support four children. And I had no desire to pull them out of their familiar routines during such a stressful time. They were young, but they were aware of the trauma.

We wanted the kids to hear about what had happened from us, but, the day after Mike confessed to me was Halloween and the kids were planning on going trick-or-treating. My parents fed the kids supper and got them dressed in their costumes, and Mike and I somehow forced our feet to walk from house to house with them. We fought in whispers standing in the street as the kids knocked on neighbor's doors. Thankfully, gathering candy was a large enough distraction that they didn't notice our lack of interest in the holiday.

After their buckets were full of candy, we took them home and asked them to sit on the couch. We had agreed to keep the conversation as blunt as possible while still age appropriate.

"I have something to tell you," Mike said somberly. Even though they were woozy with candy energy, Mike's tone alarmed them enough to sit still. "I've done something terrible, and I need to tell you about it. When I married your mom, I made a promise. I vowed that I would treat her special and I would never treat anyone else the same, special way I treat her. I broke that vow. I treated someone else the way I should only treat your mom. I am very sorry," Mike's voice faded and broke. His face contorted with effort to stop his tears.

"It's okay Daddy," Makenna said.

"No, Honey," Mike answered. "It is not okay. What I did was very wrong. And the worst part is that what I did will affect you guys. We are going to have to find a different church, and your mom is going to be pretty sad as her heart tries to heal."

"Are you going to have a divorce?" Josiah whispered.

"I can't answer that yet," I said. "But I promise that we will both love you guys with all of our hearts no matter what." We spent extra time with each of them that night as we tucked them into their beds, and their concerned faces brought tears to my eyes.

Although there were a few people who were brave enough to stand by us, we lost most of our friends. A small trickle of youth leaders made their way to our front door and told us they weren't supposed to associate with us, but their grace was a lifeline to us. Some of them gave us money, some prayed with us, some offered babysitting, and some just sat and cried with us. I think there will be a special reward in heaven for them. I've asked God for that anyway.

One benefit of losing most of my friends when I was at my most vulnerable was I didn't have to listen to a lot of different opinions. Everyone has an opinion when something terrible happens. They talk about what should be done, why this appalling thing happened, and what they would do if it happened to them. I've done it, too. I distinctly remember telling Mike early in our marriage that if he ever cheated on me, like a friend of ours had done to his wife, I would kick him out immediately and never speak to him again. We go around saying these things like we know ourselves. We don't. We don't have a clue who we are or what we would do until we find ourselves standing in the center of the rubble.

Therefore, I found myself with only a very few people to talk to as I walked through what was left of my life. One great friend, Tricia, lived out of state, but she called as soon as she heard the news.

"I didn't see it coming," I sobbed into the phone.

"You didn't have any suspicions?" she asked.

"None. I completely believed everything was fine. We had fights now and then, but no more or less than any average couple. I knew that his job was very stressful for him, and raising kids kept us pretty exhausted, but whenever we fought, I knew that we would work it out in the end. I never doubted we could resolve anything. I was still very in love. In fact, I put together a playlist with songs that reminded me of him or things we have done, and I've been playing it in my car for the last month. Mike was a hero to me, and whatever the song was about, I would picture Mike and me as the characters. That is how clueless I was."

I spoke to her almost daily after that. When I mentioned to her that I didn't know what to do about my future—if I should file for divorce, start looking for jobs and daycare, or pack the kids and drive to Alaska—she suggested I save the big decisions for later and concentrate on surviving for the time being. I am convinced that this single piece of advice saved me from a great many bad decisions.

I concentrated on just making it from one day to the next, but I found that to be too overwhelming. I then concentrated on just making it from one moment to the next. Even that was too much at times. Walking up the steps with an armload of toys was too much. On several occasions, I spent hours in a crumpled ball halfway up the steps.

Sometimes it takes all the courage we can muster to survive the space between blinks.

MIKE'S JOURNAL
11/6/2004

My day began with prayer and the overwhelming feeling that there is no way I will be able to make it to the end of this day. It seems much too long and heavy.

I let Sharla do and say anything she wants or needs to. Some of her actions give me hope that our family might make it through this intact, but 100 percent of her words are hopeless and hurtful. All the hurt needs to come out of her, and I decided to let it spill all over me. I will not defend myself or argue—even when she accuses me of things I actually did not do. It is an honor to be with her, and if a punching bag is what she needs, I will gladly be that for her.

CONFESSION

"Why did you confess to me?" I asked Mike. "You had denied the truth of the letter, and I believed you. So why confess?"

Mike sighed heavily. I had been grilling him for hours, and we were both crying and exhausted. "I couldn't stand watching you defend me." He didn't bother wiping the tears from his face, but let them drip off his chin and onto his shirt. "When I saw that, I kept wishing I was worthy of it. I wanted to be who you thought I was, and I knew that kind of man would take responsibility for his failures. So that is what I did. I should have just admitted it from the beginning."

About a week after he had told me the letter was true, I finally felt ready to hear everything that had happened in its entirety. My parents had the kids overnight, which was good because our conversation lasted many hours and reached epic volumes. Because he told me I could ask anything and he would answer honestly, I bombarded him with questions. Just to be sure I knew everything, I asked about his entire life, even things that I had known before but hadn't been worried about. He was answering honestly, and most of it wasn't new information to me. But when he began talking about the past seven months, the things he told me shocked me. I actually paused our conversation to take a short nap before hearing any more.

"Do you realize how many people you've hurt?" I screamed at him after resuming our painful discussion.

"Everyone I've ever cared about," he told me, rubbing his blood-shot eyes.

"And you ripped my babysitter away from me. She was like my sister, and I miss her, and missing her makes me even more mad," I yelled, stomach roiling. "You've devastated her and her parents, and they were nothing but good to us."

"It's terrible, I know," he said covering his face with his hands. "I can see now how despicably I behaved, and I'm repulsed by myself. I'm horrified when I think of the damage I caused that family."

"I don't know how you can ever make it right," I shouted.

"I know," he said, breaking into sobs. "I wrote an apology to each person in that family, but the church told me that I shouldn't deliver them. They asked that I break off all communication, so I don't know how I can ever apologize. I've destroyed everything."

"I need a break," I said and headed to the TV. Halfway through an episode of M*A*S*H my stomach turned to molten lava as a new thought struck me.

"Was there ever anyone else this happened with?" I whispered to Mike, who was sitting on the floor waiting for me to resume our conversation.

"No, there wasn't anyone else ever."

"Don't lie."

"I'm not lying. There wasn't ever anyone else."

And then an even worse thought struck me. "What if she's pregnant?"

"There is no chance of that," Mike answered. "There was never any intercourse."

My mind latched onto that and used it like a blanket to keep the truth from cutting so deeply.

"So it wasn't sex?"

"It wasn't intercourse, but it was sexual contact," he corrected. "It was just as wrong."

"I don't know how this whole thing works." I sighed. "I know what you've done is illegal. So what happens now? Why aren't you in jail?"

"It takes time to be charged with a crime. They will find me soon and arrest me, or I can turn myself in and confess. Either way, I need a lawyer."

"Oh, good. I was wondering where to put all our extra money."

"I'm sorry."

"Don't even say that," I shouted. "It is too small of a word to do any good."

NEW JOB

"You know how you said that you didn't want me to work with any female ever again?" Mike asked me two days later.

"Yes," I nodded.

"Well, I think I have a solution. I know it isn't enough, but Steve called and told me they are hiring in the lumberyard. I just have to interview, but I can probably get the job if I want it. It pays ten fifty an hour. It is not nearly enough, but it is something rather than nothing. And all the girls work inside in other departments. I would be working outside loading lumber. It is hard labor, and it's cold in the winter and hot in the summer, so it usually ends up being guys that work out there. What do you think?"

I thought about it for a moment. "Well, it sounds surprisingly perfect. But do you know anything about lumber?"

"Not a thing. But I sense that I suddenly have a new interest in all things timber."

"I'll have to go to Goodwill and get you some flannel shirts."

"I've also been thinking that I should sell some of our stuff. I could go through the attic and the garage and list items on eBay. We wouldn't make a lot, but we might make something. I don't want you to sell any of your stuff," Mike told me. "But we can sell some of mine.

I have really nice skis, and I have some old baseball cards that might be worth something."

"It's worth a try I guess," I agreed. "I can take pictures of the stuff you find so you can list it."

"Thank you," Mike said as he reached for my hand and then quickly pulled back realizing I would not appreciate his touch. "Also, I've been wanting to ask you a question. I know I messed up our lives and nothing I can do could ever make up for that. But is there anything I can do to make you feel better in any way at all? Is there anything you want me to stop doing or start doing? Is there anything you want me to get for you or anything you want me to get rid of? I know that whatever I do will not make things right, but I'd do anything you ask if it would just help you feel even a little bit better."

"There is one thing." I sighed, rubbing my temples with my fingertips.

"What is it?" Mike sat on the floor on his knees in front of me, eyes blazing with hope.

"If it were remotely possible, I'd want to move. I'd move somewhere far away and start fresh. With or without you, I'm not sure. Without a job, though, and with four kids, moving is out of the question. But, there are some things that I see every day that I now associate with these horrible feelings I have. One of them, besides this house, is your red Jeep. We bought it when we moved here, and it might be ridiculous, but every time I see it, I feel as if I've been slapped in the face. I hate that Jeep. I know we can't afford to get another car right now, so I haven't said anything about it. I just hate seeing it."

Mike nodded. "I totally understand. I will put it up for sale tonight, and you will never see it again."

"What will you drive? We got a great deal on that and can't afford anything else."

"Leave that up to me. Also, I think we should redecorate the house. You're right—we can't really move. But we can make this house look different. You are here with the kids all day every day. I don't want you to spend that much time being reminded of something painful. We can sell all of our furniture and paint every room. We can be creative and find inexpensive ways to make this house look completely different. Would you like that?"

"I would," I said. A warm feeling of relief spread through me. Dread that I hadn't realized I was carrying lifted, and a sense of excitement sprouted in my heart. "I think I would like that a lot."

I never did see that Jeep again.

MIKE'S JOURNAL
11/7/2004

Today I thought I would lose my mind. The stress is so high; the hatred toward me is so strong. I knew I couldn't handle any more, and I felt my mind slipping. I was a wreck, and I begged God to take my life.

Then I began to sing songs and think about God, and somehow the weight of everything began to lift.

However, the despair is only a breath away. I am only one thought away from devastation.

I fight with my emotions constantly. God, I need you to carry me.

CONVERSATIONS WITH KIDS

Morning was the worst time of the day. Sleep brought a delicious oblivion that shattered when I opened my eyes. As I yawned and stretched, wave after wave of forgotten reality crushed me until my only desire was to sink deeper into the mattress and cover my head with the darkness of the soft blankets.

Children, though, do not sit quietly and give you space and time to deal with your heartbreak and depression. They need to be bathed and fed; they need lunches to take to school. Even more demanding, they need to be lovingly disciplined and listened to. I knew there was no way I could do it, and yet I was the only option.

Sometimes I would find myself at the end of a day wondering how I had made it through the endless minutes between morning and bedtime. The prior hours melded into vague fuzzy memories, and I felt an exhausting sense of alarm wondering if I had neglected something important. I know now that I overlooked many duties, but Mike was silently covering my tracks for me. He quietly filled brown bags with lunches and placed them on the counter so they were ready for the kids to grab. He did the laundry and let me believe that I had done it. He vacuumed and told the kids bedtime stories like he wasn't drowning in his own despair. And he finally fixed the leaky bathroom faucet, the squeaky step, and the wobbly ceiling fan that we had grown used to.

"Everybody get into bed and I will be up in five minutes to tuck you in," I told the kids one night when Mike was working the late shift. When I was alone during bedtime, we had a different routine. I couldn't tell the elaborate stories Mike came up with, but I sang them their bedtime song and prayed with them, and even though they were getting older, they still liked our routine. I finished taking pictures of a board game and a tent Mike wanted to list on eBay and ten minutes later walked upstairs to the usual flurry of children running for their bed and pretending to be waiting for me.

"All right, Emery." I smiled even though I tried to look stern. "You're first tonight."

"Mommy," she said, her voice choked up, "I love you so much." To my shock, her cheeks were wet with tears.

"Emery! What's wrong, honey?" I sat on her bed and held her close to me. I wondered if she was reacting to the stress between Mike and me and worried that she might have overheard some of the heated comments I randomly lobbed at Mike like grenades.

"I don't have any reason to cry!" She wailed into my shirt. "Sometimes I just get tired, and I start to cry."

"Are you pretty tired now, sweetheart?" I asked, smoothing her hair out of her face.

"Yeah, but I don't think that is why I am crying." She sniffled and wiped her eyes. "I think I just don't have a control system!"

I smiled, trying to hold back a laugh. "Well, children sometimes have a hard time finding their control system. But this is a stressful time for all of us, and you are doing just fine. I don't think you really need to worry about that right now. Why don't we get you tucked in so you can go to sleep?"

"Yeah," she agreed, lying down. "I'm super-duper sleepy."

I said her prayers, sang her song, tucked her covers around her the way she liked, and then I kissed her on her forehead. As I was about to leave her room, she whispered, "Mommy?"

"What?"

"I know who I am, and I like myself, so I am fine with the fact that I am not good at dancing." Then her eyes slid shut and she was asleep.

When I walked into the boys' room, Josiah asked, "Hey, Mom, are you making more money with our computer?"

"I'm going to try to," I answered as I sat down on the side of his bed.

"How much money have you made us so far?"

"If you stop bouncing on your bed and lie down, I'll tell you."

"Okay," he grumbled as he crawled under the covers.

"We've made almost five hundred dollars. Can you believe that?"

"Five hundred dollars? That's like a million dollars!"

"Let's hope so. Now, stop wiggling or you'll pull your sheet off your mattress."

"Daddy told me he sells his stuff so you can watch us and we won't have to go to a babysitter."

"He did?"

"Yeah," Josiah nodded. "He said he wants to sell enough things so you can have no worries."

"He said that?"

"Yeah. So am I ever going to have a little brother or sister?" he asked.

"No," I said, maybe a little too loudly. "Two boys and two girls make a perfect family. We are lucky."

"But I would like a little brother," Drake said from his side of the room.

"Well, what if you got a sister instead?" I asked, sure that thought would shut down this conversation.

Josiah hesitated, face scrunched in deep thought. "Well, she would probably be really cute and fun." He tapped his chin with his finger a few times and then decided, "I would be nice to her."

"I know you would, honey," I agreed as I lightly spread the sheet across his body. I had discovered that he didn't like being hot as he slept, so I bunched his comforter at the foot of the bed and made sure to leave the sheet untucked so he could stick his feet out. "But your dad and I are done having children."

"Why?" Drake asked as I laid a heavy blanket on him and tucked it snugly all around him. "Are you guys neutered?"

"Kind of." I laughed. "But more than that, we are just really happy with you guys and don't feel like we need any more children. Now, it is long past your bedtime, so let me finish your prayers so you guys can go to sleep."

Still chuckling to myself, I left the boys' room after their prayers were finished and found Makenna already sound asleep. I straightened her blanket, turned off her light, and just looked at her sweet, innocent face. Her blond hair almost glowed in the moonlight streaming through her window, and the expression on her face was so worry-free it almost hurt to look at. She looked like an angel, and I knew that in spite of everything, I was blessed.

MIKE'S JOURNAL
11/9/2004

S in works like this: It baited me in with a tiny compromise—a deluded line of reasoning only slightly veering from the truth. Then I tried to fix my folly in the shadows of my own heart. The reasons for keeping it hidden were logical—it will hurt my wife, my family, my friends. Nobody understands. I thought I could correct it before any real damage was done. But the more I tried to fix it, the more it controlled me. Like trying to wipe sap off my hands, every place I touched attempting to clean became dirty with the stickiness of the sin, and the shadow grew. Then, the shadow, that seemed at one time to be a place of refuge, became, instead, a dark pit of despair, and I drowned in it.

NEIGHBORHOOD CONFESSION

"Where were you?" I asked Mike as he walked through the front door. I had seen him return home from work, but then he disappeared for almost an hour.

"I've been talking to our neighbors. I'm pretty sure my story will be on the news soon, and I wanted all the neighbors to hear it from me first."

"So you just walked up to people's houses and told them what's going on?"

"Yep." Mike rubbed his hands down his face.

"That had to be hard."

"One of the hardest things I've ever done."

"How did people respond?"

"Differently. The Browns offered to help in any way they could. They want to drop off food, and they will babysit anytime. Most people just thanked me for letting them know. Brad said he's done worse things and was surprised I felt that I needed to tell him. Cliff said I was a bad man."

"He did?" Cliff was our elderly neighbor whose yard always made ours look shabby.

"Yeah. He said he was tempted several times to cheat on his wife and never did. Then he said I was bad."

"What did you say?"

"I told him I know that, but I still wanted him to hear it from me since we are neighbors. I told him I'm sorry I did it, and I'm sorry for the effect it will have on our neighborhood."

When the nightly news featured a picture of my husband, my humiliation was complete. I knew Mike had talked to his lawyer a couple of times, but the system surprised me with its slowness. I guess from watching movies, I had assumed that the bad guy goes to prison almost immediately after the crime is committed. In reality, the process drags out while the lawyers communicate back and forth. During that unendurable, suspenseful time, our emotions swung like a pendulum between panic and peace.

I believe the court system tries to make things fair and make people pay for the wrongs they have done in a financial or practical way, but when has that ever made anyone really feel better? And because both sides have lawyers advising them not to talk to the other side, nobody talks it out, heals emotionally, or gets over it.

It only got worse after that. I grew to dread the ringing of the phone. We were plagued by reporters, angry church members, and much more dangerous people. One day as I unloaded groceries into the refrigerator, the phone rang. Panic coursed through my body and caused my scalp to tingle. I took a deep breath and told myself I was being unreasonable.

"Hello," I managed.

"Sharla Hintz? This is Detective Barnes with the FBI."

"Oh."

"Your husband's name has come to our attention, and we would like to ask you a few questions concerning a trip he took awhile ago to Afghanistan."

"That was a trip he took with our church."

"Did it seem in any way suspicious to you?"

"No. Why would it? He went with a group to help people."

"Nevertheless, ma'am, Afghanistan has become an interesting travel destination, and your husband's name has begun to arouse suspicion."

Oddly, the part that scared me the most in what the detective said was that he called me *ma'am*. "That trip had nothing to do with what is going on right now."

"No offense, ma'am, but I will be the judge of that. I will be in contact if I need any more information."

With trembling hands, I hung up the phone and realized that I had been right to dread answering it. I glared at the plastic traitor and told myself that it couldn't get much worse than that, but two days later it did.

IT GETS WORSE

"Hello?" I whispered in to the phone.

"Mrs. Hintz? My name is Sandy, and I work with the Department of Human Services. Because of the situation your family is involved in, I need to talk to you and your husband and meet your children. Is there a time I could visit you at your house?"

"Why do you need to meet my children?" I asked as I sank to the floor.

"When a situation of this nature comes to our attention, we like to investigate the home of any children involved. We need to meet the children and ask them some questions about what goes on at home and if they feel safe."

"My kids are safe," I murmured.

"Of course. However, I will be stopping by. Will everybody be home tomorrow evening at seven?"

"Yes."

"I will see you then."

I sat on the floor in a heap, as if my bones had been removed, until I heard voices in the front yard. I glanced at the clock and realized school was over. I plastered a smile on my face and robotically gathered something edible for the after-school snack I usually had prepared. Thankfully, the kids were too young to realize that carrots and peanut butter didn't go together, so they dipped the carrots in the peanut butter and cheerfully chatted about their day as the robot version of me smiled at them and didn't hear a word they said.

"Mommy, let me go!" Josiah said.

"What? Oh, sorry," I said as I realized I was hugging him tightly.

He popped the last peanut butter covered carrot into his mouth and hopped across the kitchen floor to his backpack. He unzipped it and proudly waved a packet in the air. "I have homework like big kids!"

"Why are you crying, Mommy?" Makenna asked full of concern.

"What? Am I crying?" I felt my cheeks and realized they were wet. "Oh, um, I just remembered a sad story. I'm fine though. I think I just have to go to the bathroom." I felt the flood of tears coming and knew I couldn't let the kids witness a breakdown. I opened the front door and walked into the front yard thinking that the cold air might stem off the tidal wave threatening to overtake me.

"Mommy!" Makenna yelled, "You can't go to the bathroom in the yard! I got in big trouble for that! Remember? If you go potty in the yard you get a time-out!"

"Oh, yeah." I laughed too loudly. "Thanks for the warning."

Every action felt foggy and surreal until the next evening. When I heard a knock on the door, every detail suddenly settled into sharp focus. Noises were too loud and lights were too bright.

"Hello, I am Sandy," a stout older woman said as she marched through the front door. A pimple-faced kid, who was probably much older than he looked, sneaked past her and disappeared into the house. Sandy told me his name and what he was doing, but I couldn't concentrate or understand what she said because her voice was so loud. I thought about asking her to speak more quietly but realized the problem was probably in my head since nobody else thought she was shouting. The kids came running like they always did when we had a visitor, and Sandy soon had them sitting on the ground in front of her like they were at school.

"All right, children. I have some questions to ask you and I want you to answer honestly. Just say the first thing that comes into your mind and don't worry. You will not get in trouble for any answer you give me. I just want you to be honest. Can you do that?"

"Yes, Miss Sandy!" they shouted in unison.

"What is your favorite color?"

Makenna's hand shot up and she shouted, "Pink!"

"Good! What is your dog's name?"

"Canaan!" they all shouted slightly out of sync.

"This is an important one. Do you like being home?"

"Yes."

"Do you feel safe at home?"

"Yes."

"Is there anything at home your dad doesn't want you to look at?"

Everybody except Drake shook their heads.

"Drake, is there something you are thinking of?"

"Yes."

"Can you tell me or show me what it is?"

Drake ran out of the room as I held my breath and glared at Mike who looked oddly calm and slightly puzzled. A moment later Drake ran into the room with a sheet of paper and shoved it at Sandy. After glancing over the paper she asked, "Your dad doesn't like for you to look at the bank statement?"

"No, *he* doesn't like to look at it. It makes him frown."

"Now, that I can relate to," Sandy mumbled, and her stern face threatened to grin.

The questions went on for ten more minutes before Sandy took each child aside and spoke to them individually. Then she sat with us at the kitchen table while the kids scattered away to watch *Blue's Clues.*

"Mrs. Hintz, has your husband ever threatened you or scared you in any way?"

"No. Never."

"Before this incident, was there a history of affairs or promiscuity?"

"No."

"Have you ever seen pornography in your house or noticed it on your computer?"

"No. Never."

The pimple-faced kid, who I had completely forgotten existed, returned and handed Sandy a sheet of paper. She read it quickly and then stared at me as if she was trying to look at my soul.

"I'm going to be honest with you. You seem like a very loving, concerned mother. As far as that goes, Mr. Hintz, you seem like a very loving, concerned father. We have already spoken to all of your babysitters, some family members, and close friends. All of them have reported nothing but good things about this family. There are a lot of people in and out of your house, and none of them report ever finding pornography. Jack has thoroughly checked all of your computers, and there is no pornographic activity on any of them, erased or otherwise. Your children are well adjusted, respectful, and content. I do not see anything here to worry about.

"However, I will offer you a word of advice." She leaned forward and her eyes bored into mine over the top rim of her glasses. "Don't let people who are not family members into the inner circle of your family. It gets too complicated, and the lines get too easy to cross."

"I can promise you," I said with feeling, "that will never happen again."

"Not only will it never happen again," Mike said, "I couldn't regret more that it ever happened in the first place. I was an idiot. A complete and utter idiot. I'm so sorry that you had to come here and do this, and if my wife can ever forgive me, I will never put my family in a position like this again."

"Well, Jack," Sandy said to the computer tech as she gathered her things and stood up, "we should buy a lottery ticket on the way home. The planets must all be aligned just perfectly because in thirty-seven years of doing this job, today is the first time I have heard an apology."

MIKE'S JOURNAL
11/15/2005

I cannot begin to let myself think of what tomorrow holds—that is too much to bear. Every day seems longer than the day before.

SEX OFFENDER

"Bruce is no longer alive," I said, solemnly. I had been thinking over the conversation from weeks earlier in which my mom had told me that I needed to ease into bad news. When I had told her bluntly that my old school friend was dead, she reacted with strong emotional shock and told me that I shouldn't announce bad news so directly. I decided I needed practice. I had tried about twenty different ways to state that someone was dead, and I was watching to see which way caused the least distress.

"How did Bruce die?" Makenna asked gravely from the end of the couch.

"That's not important. Did that last way sound any better?"

"What if, since he is a bear, Bruce died from getting stung by bees when he tried to steal their honey?"

"Okay, he died from bees."

"Try again."

"Bruce was in a terrible bee accident and suffered so much that he finally died."

"But, since Bruce is a stuffed bear, the bees probably couldn't hurt him."

"Maybe they had magic stinging potion that works on stuffed animals. But did that way sound any better?"

"Maybe you should just say, 'If you want to see your dear friend who is a sweetheart, Bruce, then you should do it with Jesus in heaven because that is where he went after the bees got finished with him.'"

"Oh, Dad is home!" I said when I heard a car pull into the driveway. "Run to bed!"

"I will be as quiet as a fairy ninja," Makenna whispered as she bolted upstairs on tip-toe.

The lawyer had explained that Mike would most likely be required to register as a sex offender in the state of Iowa regardless of the outcome of the impending trial. People who are put on the sex offender registry are required to attend therapy. After talking it over, Mike decided that he would like to volunteer to get started in counseling right away rather than wait for the court to order it. He thought it would probably be a good thing, even if he didn't end up being required to do it. It was his first night, and I was extremely curious about it.

"How did it go?" I asked Mike when he walked in the door.

"It was the most surreal thing I've ever done. It's hard to even explain." He threw his jacket across the arm of the couch and sat down heavily, scrubbing his face with his hands.

"Did you meet your counselor?"

"Oh yeah. Dan. He's the scariest person I've ever encountered."

"Really?" I asked, surprised. "Aren't counselors supposed to be compassionate and understanding?"

"If you picture in your mind the typical counselor with peaceful eyes and a soft voice," Mike said, leaning forward, elbows on his knees, "this guy is the exact opposite. I don't get intimidated by people very easily, but I am already dreading the next time I have to see Dan."

"What is so intimidating about him?" I asked, rubbing my eyes. Mike had left just after supper and it was nearly eleven by the time he got home. I had put the kids to bed, but Makenna and curiosity had kept me awake.

"Well, first of all, the situation is just plain scary. I walked in, and there was this room full of about twenty-five guys all sitting in folding chairs in a circle. The counselor and the probation officer that works with these guys, who is a woman by the way, sat together. So the probation officer, Meg, is the only woman there. Then we had to go around and say what we did and why we are in treatment. I had to write my statement tonight. You can read it," he said, offering me a piece of marked up paper.

Taking a deep breath, I braced myself and read, "My victim was a seventeen –year-old member of my youth group. Over a seven month period I engaged in sexual activity with my victim that included kissing and fondling, stopping short of intercourse. I am in treatment because I deeply desire to understand the patterns and triggers that caused me to violate my own ethical standards and cause such pain to so many people. I want to put roadblocks in the way of that ever happening again in my life. I will do anything to avoid reoffending again."

"It's weird that one little paragraph can symbolize so much damage." I felt ridiculed by the short sentences. So much pain seemed to necessitate volumes of words, and the curt synopsis seemed to mock me.

"We had to be able to clearly state our crime as succinctly as possible. Stating it concisely doesn't allow for deflecting blame or minimizing what we've done. We are allowed more words when we state why we are in therapy. I'll read it at each meeting for the rest of the time I'm in the program. So, that's what the other guys did tonight. And, any time Dan or Meg felt like a guy wasn't telling the whole truth or minimizing part of it, one of them would lambaste that guy. Seriously lambaste."

"What do you mean?" I asked. "Like yell at the guy or something?"

"Yeah, that and threaten them."

"Threaten to throw him out of the group?"

"No. Threaten to send him to jail."

"What? They can do that?"

"They can and they did. It happened tonight. A guy was telling his story, and Dan felt that the guy was not taking enough responsibility.

It's confidential, so I can't tell you his name, but I'm pretty sure I can tell you what happened. He is being charged with statutory rape, but he was saying that they were both drunk. Dan felt like the guy was using the drinking as an excuse for why he had done what he did. So Dan stopped him and told him to tell it again without pushing blame away from himself. But the second time through, the guy said that he had sex with a woman he met in a bar, which implies mutual consent. He didn't say that he had raped her, which was minimizing his crime. So Dan called the police, and they came and put him in handcuffs and dragged him off to jail."

"What? Just like that?" I was having a hard time comprehending such a scenario. "Will he be back?"

"I don't know. Nobody seemed surprised by what was happening."

"Yeah, I can see how that would be a bit frightening." I pictured the scene in my head and a shiver ran down my spine. "What were the other guys there like? Were they scary?"

"Everyone was at a different place in his treatment. Some of the newer guys were defensive and angry, but some of the guys who had been there longer just seemed like normal guys. The newer guys didn't want to tell their story because they were scared Dan would send them to jail, but the veteran guys didn't want to tell their story because they were ashamed."

"Do you think they were really ashamed, or had they just learned to play along so Dan would leave them alone?"

"Well, it was my first night, but it seemed real. I think the guys who don't progress in therapy get kicked out. The guys who make it to the end of their two years have had to let it change them. One guy actually cried, which is not easy to do in a room full of criminals and a terrifying, jail-happy counselor."

"Two years just doesn't seem long enough for a crime like rape."

"Well, there is a wide spectrum of crimes. You've got some of the less harmful crimes, like peeing in a park or streaking on a college campus. Then there are really weird situations like a seventeen-year-old guy who had sex with his fifteen-year-old girlfriend. They are actually still together, too. She even called Dan and told him she had given consent, but because of her age, it is considered abuse. Then there is a whole lot of the stuff you hear about on the news: stalking, threatening, raping. Then some guys are at the other end of the spectrum, which I can't tell you about because it makes me want to throw up."

"Oh."

"I actually learned things tonight that I had never in my life wondered about before. I feel like I want to scrub my brain with Clorox."

"So those guys, the ones who make you want to throw up, are they only in there for two years as well?"

"Well, some of those guys have already been in prison for a long time and did treatment there. Now they are required to do two more years of sex-offender treatment on the outside because they have served their time and are ready to be released."

"Was there anyone else just starting?"

"A couple. I talked to one guy, Rob, for a while afterward."

"What did he do?"

"I can't tell you that because I just told you his name. I can tell you the types of things guys are in there for, but not specifically who did what."

"That makes sense."

"I can tell you, though, that Rob is in a hard situation. His family cut him off when he got arrested. He doesn't have anywhere to go. He has to give Meg an address, but he doesn't have one. He lost his job when he was arrested, and now he can't afford a deposit to rent a place. If he doesn't get an address by next week, he will go to jail."

"Maybe he should move out of town."

"He has to be able to attend weekly therapy meetings, so he can't go too far. Also, Dan kept saying how important it was for all of us to find support from friends or family. He said the worst thing is to become isolated because people in isolation have no accountability or hope. They feel alone, which makes them depressed and desperate, and desperate people do desperate things. He doesn't want us moving out to some deserted place and losing contact with people we care about. But the people Rob cares about have already ceased contact with him."

"What is he going to do?"

"I don't know. But it makes me so thankful that I have had a place to live. Thank you. Thank you for letting me live here and not cutting me off yet. I know you can still do that, and I wouldn't blame you. In fact, after tonight, I am even more shocked that you didn't kick me to the curb yet. If I belong in that group of guys, I don't belong with someone like you. So thank you."

CONFLICTING EMOTIONS

"You okay?" Tricia's voice said over the phone.

"I'm doing what you said and just surviving moment to moment."

"That is good enough. You are doing great." It was good to hear her voice and nice to know she cared.

"I don't leave the house very often," I confessed.

"Why not?"

"People recognize me. Everybody thinks I should just file for divorce, and they think I am stupid to wait so long. I heard people talking about it while I was checking out at the grocery store. In fact, someone followed me around Wal-Mart. I didn't realize it, but a security guard alerted me to the situation. He pointed out someone I don't really know but recognize from our church. The security guard had to walk beside me as I finished up, and then he escorted me to my car to make sure I was safe."

"That's pretty freaky." Her concerned voice brought tears to my eyes.

"Yeah."

"Listen, nobody else has the right to make this decision for you. People say a lot of things, but you never know what you will actually do until you are the one in the situation facing the consequences on either side of a choice," Tricia assured me.

"That is true." Nobody understood all the factors, and nobody else had to answer for this decision or live with the consequences.

"What made you decide to marry Mike in the first place?" she asked.

"Well, I loved him, of course." I thought for a moment. "But I made the decision before he even asked me. I was in a friend's bedroom, and she had quotes and poems taped to her wall. I was struggling at the time trying to decide how much to commit to our relationship; I didn't want to lose my friendship with Lori. Then I read something she had written out. It was a verse from the Bible that said, 'Two are better than one. If one falls the other can reach out and help. A person standing alone can be attacked and defeated, but two can stand back to back and conquer. And three are even better for a triple braided cord is not easily broken.' I wanted to be like that triple-braided cord with Mike and God. But now that cord feels like a noose."

Mike began work at the lumberyard at five every morning, but when he returned home he helped me with my housework as if it were a privilege. I sometimes yelled at him, and I oftentimes cut him down with hurtful comments. He never defended himself.

"Robert, your friend from high school, stopped by today with his family, and also Cliff came over," I told Mike as he swept the kitchen floor. He still wore his lumberyard uniform, and the smell of sawed wood filled the kitchen. I watched his muscular shoulders and strong arms as he pushed the tiny broom around the linoleum floor, and I pictured in my mind the stack of lumber I had seen him load onto a truck at noon when I dropped off a thermos of hot chocolate. The guys working with him stared, mouths agape, when he handled the wood as if it were construction paper instead of construction lumber. He loaded stack after stack without even a grimace, muscles bulging from his neck, shoulders, and arms. I had always found his brawny appearance attractive, and I had to rub my eyes to get the appealing image out of my mind. How could I be attracted to him and, at the same time, be repulsed by the thought of being near him? I felt like my conflicting emotions were going to rip my mind from my heart, my body from my soul.

"Really? You've had a lot of company. What did everybody say?"

"Cliff asked if you could clean out his gutters." Cliff, our next-door neighbor, was getting too old to maintain his house in the manner he was used to, and Mike usually offered to do the things Cliff could no longer do. "Robert and his family dropped off some groceries and just wanted to be nice. It was really kind. It gave me hope that we still might have some friends. They mentioned, though, that the phone book has our number under my name only. Your name isn't with mine."

"Is it usually listed like that?"

"No. It is probably a sign."

Mike didn't answer, but I saw the pain in his face before he turned back to his sweeping.

He was riddled with repentance and remorse, but he had ruined every aspect of my life. He would have given me anything I asked for, but there was nothing I wanted that would make up for what he had done. I turned to walk away, but in my mind I saw a cord. It was frayed and damaged, and I knew that it was very weak. I knew that it was the cord I had spoken to Tricia about earlier, and I knew that my choices would decide whether that cord fell apart or survived.

I remembered as a newlywed thinking that we were a team. I wanted to be the kind of person who would stand and fight next to my husband when he fell down, like the verse from the Bible said. How could I do that, though, when I couldn't even stand being in the same room as him?

MIKE'S JOURNAL
11/20/2005

I remember when I wanted to have more hours in the days so I could get more done, but now I only wish they were shorter. To wake up in the morning is like looking at a road that goes straight uphill and runs out of sight.

LEFT

A bright light captured my attention as I dumped the lunch dishes into the sink. The sunshine streaming in the window reflected off the diamond in my wedding ring causing bursts of light to flash around the kitchen. I stared at the gold band with the small flower-shaped diamond and felt it mocking me. The burden of reality crushed me, suffocating me, and I couldn't breathe. My ring had become a gallows strangling the life from me.

I tore at it violently, attempting to rip it from my finger. When it wouldn't slide off, I scraped at it and scratched at it with my nails until lines of red blood ran down the sink, crisscrossing the white porcelain like veins. When the ring finally let go and clinked against the bottom of the sink, I noticed my finger was covered with bloody scratches and gouges. It looked better to me that way.

Mike turned into the driveway on his bicycle as I was carrying a suitcase to the minivan. His red Jeep had sold quickly, and he had been riding his bike since then even though the temperature was below freezing most mornings. He leaned the bike against the side of the house and walked toward me as if he were approaching a wild tiger.

He smelled of sawed wood, and hours of sliding lumber had sculpted his arms and shoulders, which I tried to ignore.

"I'm taking the kids and going to my parents' house," I announced as I returned to the living room for the box of toys I had packed. The kids were already in the car waiting in their car seats.

"Are you leaving me?" Mike asked, following me inside the house and speaking softly so the kids would not hear.

"Yes." I threw the word at him like a dagger.

"When will I see you again?" I knew he was trying to stay calm, but panic pinched his voice so it sounded thin.

"I don't know. I don't know anything. Nothing is the same; I'm not the same. I am no longer who I was, and I have no idea who I am. You have made me an anathema to myself because I hate who I have been."

I felt victorious when Mike's eyes turned red and filled with tears, but he fought to maintain his composure. Even as I detested him, I admired the strength I saw in him, which only fueled my anger.

"Marriage is the most wicked of all conspiracies," I shouted at him, "and it sours me to life."

I slammed the front door behind me, and backed the minivan out of the driveway.

"Guys, we are going on a vacation at Grandma's house." I tried to sound cheerful, but only succeeded in sounding like a cartoon. "We will be together, and we will be okay. It will be a lot of fun." They weren't paying attention, but I was mainly speaking to myself anyway.

MIKE'S JOURNAL
11/21/2004

L ife is misery; it is suffering; it is pain. The worst part of all is that I am the villain. I go to work and every person is talking about me and few are talking to me. I find it difficult to show my face. I go through my day entirely alone and then after work I listen to Sharla who is hurt and angry. I have no positive meaning to her.

   I am horrified at the wickedness that I have done and the devastation that I have wrought.

THE RISK

T he kids stabbed pumpkins with lawn darts in my parents' backyard as I sat and cried in the house. They had a campout on the living room floor, watched movies, and played games. Sometimes they sensed that I was experiencing something profoundly terrible, and they would quiet down and stare at me until I smiled. Then they would run back to their play.

A smile seems like such a small movement, but sometimes arranging your face into that shape takes all the effort one human can muster.

I wanted to forget my troubles and play with the kids, but shortly after arriving at my parents' house, I threw out my back and had to sit in a chair for two days feeling helpless and dependent. The slightest movement caused immense amounts of pain, so I was trapped with my thoughts, and my mind was churning.

"Mom, would you turn the music off?" I asked as she passed by with an armful of puzzles.

"Do you want me to change it to something else?"

"No. Music really isn't made for someone in my state. It's all about love and happiness. It's irritating."

If I hadn't been so miserable, I would have been annoyed at the consoling way she kissed the top of my head, but instead, I found it comforting.

As I sat still, I thought a lot about love. I wondered if there was any word more terrifying. I had told Mike I loved him thousands of times, and each time, what I was really saying was that I trusted him to take care of my heart. I read a quote by a man named Tim Woodsman that said, "Hearts are not practical until they have become unbreakable."

How does a heart become unbreakable when we are constantly leaving it in the care of another person? We give it to the person we love, and it is vulnerable. Then we hold that person accountable for the care our heart receives.

It is easy this way because we have someone to blame if it all goes badly. We want someone to blame more than just about anything. Also, we get to let someone else do the hard work of maintaining our happiness and well-being. We convince ourselves that our happiness is our lover's responsibility. We enter into a relationship believing that the other person will complete us or meet our needs. It feels really great to believe that someone else is responsible for making us happy. This, though, is not how it works. Someone else can never complete us; love cannot fulfill us unless we are already complete.

I think people say they are in love, but what they are calling love is really something else. They probably mean attraction, infatuation, or respect. They mean some utterly understandable emotion instead of love. These emotions feel nice and they tuck us into an illusion in which we feel protected and special because someone *loves* us. We believe that our lover would never hurt us because loving us is his or her job.

We don't understand that this illusion is dangerous and that as long as we live in it, we are not safe. As long as our well-being rests in someone else's hands, we are not safe.

True love is not understandable. It is intended to strip us of our selfishness and strip us of our needs. It is scary for us to remove the responsibility of our completeness from somebody else because then we have to place it on ourselves. We have to do the hard work of being a complete person and maintaining our own well-being. When we do that, our heart becomes unbreakable. Other people can cause pain, confusion, remorse, but they cannot truly break us.

We have it backward. We should not use love to complete us; we should be complete and then we are free to love.

One counselor, Bob Paul, explained it to me another way. He said that we often enter a relationship because we feel that we *need* that other person. We need them for many reasons. We need them to make us feel happy, or we need them to complete us, or we can't live without them. Whatever the reason may be, the extent to which we *need* that person is the extent to which we are not free to *love* them. *Need* and *love* are not the same thing. Need is selfish; love is selfless.

In fact, we shouldn't really *need* anyone. It is only when we admit that we *want* that other person that we are free to love them. If we *want* someone, we are able to live without them but choose them anyway.

It is important to realize that choosing to allow someone access to our vulnerabilities will cause conflict and will sometimes feel bad. The relationship will take effort and will, at times, be troubling, even devastating. Along with great joy, we will experience great pain. That is the risk. The only safe way to live with such a great risk is to realize that we choose the risk willingly, and if the unthinkable happens, we will also choose our next step willingly. We are not trapped, and we will survive.

MIKE'S JOURNAL
11/24/2004

Today I went to visit Sharla and the kids. I miss them all so much.

I saw Sharla, and I wanted to kiss and hold and touch her. The desire was so strong that I placed my shadow so that my shadow hand could hold her shadow hand.

Then I made room in my spirit for something else—joy. I played with the kids and enjoyed every minute of it. I was so glad to be a part of their laughter. I kept looking for reasons to laugh, and it helped. It was actually a good day, and I enjoyed life more than I have for a long while.

PICK YOUR RESULT

"I played with Grandpa today, and now I know that me, a magnifying glass, and the sun can do amazing things," Emery told me as she crawled onto my lap and we snuggled in my dad's leather chair.

"And I found a pet frog today," Drake said as he walked through the room with a pancake the size of his head, "but then I accidentally peeled all his skin off so I'm gonna feed him my pancake leftover from breakfast."

"Grandpa is shy, isn't he?" Emery asked me.

"He is most definitely not shy," I told her, smiling at the thought. "He's just quiet."

"Isn't that the same thing?" She turned her head to look at me, and her wispy hair tickled my chin.

"No. Shy is being afraid of people and what they think. Grandpa isn't afraid of people."

"What is Grandpa afraid of?" she asked as she slid off my lap and ran away without waiting for the answer.

"Not one little thing," I whispered to the space she left behind.

"You're doing great, Sharla," Dad said as he dragged a chair next to mine.

"What do you mean?" I grumbled. "I'm doing terrible."

"You're making it." He took my hand and rubbed it.

"I don't know if I can make it anymore, Dad," I said, eyes filling with tears.

"Let me tell you something, honey." Although my dad's voice was always quiet, his words sounded like a roar to me. "Trials happen to everyone. They are like tests in life; they show you who you really are and what you really believe. They let you decide who you want to be and give you the opportunity to be that person. You don't get to choose what these tests are going to be. They just happen. But you *do* get to choose your reaction. It's one of the only things in life you ever really choose for yourself."

Speechless, I just looked at him silently.

"Remember that, honey." He gave my hand a final squeeze as he stood. "You don't choose your test; you only choose your result." I looked at my dad, and to me he looked like a grand lion.

"Guess what this is, Mama?" Emery interrupted our conversation, shoving a sculpture made from magnets into my face.

"Um, a horse?" I guessed.

"No."

"A fire hydrant?" my dad guessed.

"No," Emery said, forehead crinkling.

"A dragon?" I tried.

"No," she said in exasperation. "I wish someone around here was like me," she said as she spun on her heel and walked away.

It took several days of wrestling with the wisdom of my dad's statement before I was able to admit the truth of it. It seems the wisdom most needed is the very thing you would like to denounce as untrue, unfair, and outrageous. When my dad spoke to me that day, I wanted to cover my ears and pretend I had never heard what he said. It was uncomfortable, and I hated that it was true. I wanted comfort and soothing words; even pity would have been better than the sharp truth he spoke.

Truth can be a wicked friend.

I wanted the situation to work out like a scene in a movie where my dad pulled out the old shotgun and hunted Mike down with anger pouring out of his eyes. Meanwhile, my mother would baby me and lay all manner of curses upon the man who had destroyed my happiness. The kids would refuse to ever speak to their father again and we would bravely face our future like a tiny team of soldiers. I didn't want the truth; the truth feels bad.

Sometimes we think that in order to be there for someone who is suffering, we need to take their side and say nasty things about the other side. I found that unhelpful. It wasn't healthy for me to hear bad things about Mike or about the babysitter. I needed the kind of help a severely injured patient in the emergency room would need: a safe and healthy atmosphere, attention, and care. It would do no good to walk into the emergency room and tell the victim of a car crash that the patients from the other car were horrible people and deserved to suffer. It might feel momentarily nice to hear those words, but it does not lead to healing. A wounded patient needs health and truth.

I did not get babied. My parents cared for me and loved me. They helped with my workload. But as soon as my back was better, I was the one mostly taking care of the children, doing their laundry, making their lunches. Mom spoiled me by letting me sleep a little late, but she still gently insisted I change out of my pajamas and made me leave the house every now and then.

What they gave me was help, love, and a good dose of reality. They gave me a real shot at a happy future.

Two weeks later, I had made one small decision. I decided to go home. I didn't decide anything else. I still didn't know if I would file for divorce, and I didn't know how I would be able to face Mike. I knew I was experiencing a test I would never have chosen, and I knew I was the only one in charge of the result.

I didn't figure out everything, just the next thing.

MIKE'S JOURNAL
11/29/2004

We celebrated Thanksgiving separately. Sharla went to her parents' house, while I took the kids and went to my parents' house. There were around twenty people in the small kitchen, but, surrounded by my family, food, and laughter, I felt so alone. I could barely endure the holiday due to the absence of one person.

What is the meaning of a kiss? Is it something you give or something you get? Sharla asked me that question. I've been thinking about that. I remember feeling frustrated that Sharla was tired and busy. I took it as rejection. I was seeking to get kisses. I think, though, that a kiss is a giving expression of love, devotion, affection, and faithfulness. It is an act that is for the receiver that says, "This is for you—a tangible expression of my love for you."

THOUGHTFUL DELIVERY

"Good morning," I said, surprised to see Mike when I walked into the kitchen. I didn't know or care where he slept at night, and he was usually at work before I woke up in the mornings.

"A guy at work asked to trade shifts with me today," Mike explained as he heaved an old stereo onto the kitchen table. "And another guy is sick so I am working a double shift today. I'll go in two hours late, but I will stay until close."

"That will be a long day."

"Yeah, but I'll get overtime. I found some old comic books I can sell, this old stereo, and the rest of my camping supplies."

"I'll take pictures of it this morning," I told him.

"I'll move all of it before the kids wake up so you can use the table. Where would you like it?"

"Put it on the couch. The light from the front window works nicely for the pictures."

"Guess what?" Mike asked as he began loading the couch with lanterns, camping pans, and sleeping bags. "Apparently, that board game we put on eBay is a rare collector's edition. Some guy in Italy bought it. You'll never guess what it sold for."

"A hundred dollars?" I guessed.

"More."

"A hundred and fifty?"

"Seven hundred dollars!"

"What?" I yelled. "For a game? A board game that has been sitting in our basement for years?"

"I know! I was shocked," Mike said as he tugged his stocking hat over his ears preparing for a cold bike ride. "I paid all of our bills, bought all the things on your grocery list, and still had forty dollars that I put in your purse. Do whatever you want with it."

"Really?"

"Yep." He opened the front door and turned around to look at me. "You haven't done anything fun for a while. You could go to a movie or buy some new clothes. Whatever you want. I'm working till close so I probably won't see you till tomorrow. Love you."

"Love you … I mean, 'bye." I didn't want to tell him I loved him, but the habit was hard to break. I looked at my purse and saw the money sticking out of the front pocket. Smiling at the way a man organizes items in a purse, I pulled out my wallet and slid the crisp bills inside, hardly daring to believe that they were real.

As I prepared breakfast, the three older kids walked sleepily down the stairs and sat at the table. I yawned and thought about the night before. For the children's sake, Mike and I reserved our heated conversations for late at night after I was sure everybody was asleep, and they were mostly carried out with loud whispering. Last night's argument had gone very late, and my eyes felt like sandpaper due to lack of sleep. As tired as I was, I was baffled that Mike woke up hours before me searching for items to sell.

I opened the silverware drawer and rolled my eyes as a memory from the night before flooded my mind. I was shouting at Mike in my loudest possible whisper as I unloaded the dishwasher. Mike reached for the silverware to help put it away. I grabbed it away from him and told him I didn't need his help. After furiously placing the utensils where they belonged, I slammed the drawer shut. A splintering noise surprised me, and I opened the drawer to investigate what had happened. But when I pulled on the handle, the front half of the drawer fell forward and the back half didn't move. I had somehow broken the drawer in half. Astounded, I looked to see if the drawer had broken along a seam, but it hadn't. I had splintered the wooden sides of the drawer and cracked the bottom across the center.

"You'd better fix that!" I had shouted in a whisper at Mike before spinning on my heel and stomping off to bed.

Now, the drawer was sliding easily in and out, and new silver brackets braced both sides and the bottom of the drawer.

"These get screwed in with a screwdriver that needs to be plugged in," Josiah said, pointing to the silver brackets.

"How do you know that?" I asked.

"I woke up and saw Daddy working on it last night," Josiah explained as he grabbed a spoon. "Daddy let me help, and he said I was a carpet turd."

"A carpet turd?"

"Yeah. That's a guy that makes stuff with wood for his job."

"Oh! You mean a carpenter?"

"Yeah. But what happened to the drawer?"

"What did Daddy tell you?"

"He said it was his fault that it broke, but I know he didn't break it."

"How do you know that?"

"Because he was crying. So he didn't break it. And you're too little to break it."

"Maybe our silverware is too heavy," I teased him as I grabbed him and tickled his belly.

"Wake me up!" Emery called from her bed upstairs.

"You're lucky," I told Josiah. "I have to stop tickling you so I can go get your sister up."

"Can't Emery just get out of bed and come down here like the rest of us?" Josiah asked, straightening out his pajama shirt.

"Yeah, but don't tell her that," I instructed. "I think it's cute that she thinks she needs an adult to get her out of bed in the mornings."

By noon, we had played every game we own and invented a few. It was too cold to go outside, and I didn't have the energy to load everyone in the minivan and go somewhere. I counted the many hours before bedtime, and I began to panic.

"There's a strange guy at the door," Drake told me after yelling my name in rapid succession about twelve times.

"A guy you don't know, or a guy who is strange?" I asked.

"A guy I don't know."

"Then you probably shouldn't call him strange," I instructed as I heaved him onto my hip and walked to the living room.

"Hello?" I said, opening the front door.

"Hi. My name is Joe, and I work at the lumberyard with your husband, Mike."

"Oh, hi," I said, opening the door a bit wider and letting Drake out of my grip.

"I just got off work, and Mike asked if I would drop some stuff off here," Joe explained. "Apparently he rides a bike to work?"

"Yeah, he does."

"Well, I already told him he was nuts for that." Joe shrugged. "Anyway, I've got some wood, some paint, and a bunch of other stuff Mike said he would explain to you later. He said you are redecorating your house, and this is for something he is going to build."

"Thank you," I said as Joe loaded the kitchen counter with the supplies.

"He's a smart guy." Joe grunted, carrying two five-gallon buckets of paint. "He grabbed all of this stuff out of the free pile."

"The free pile?" I asked.

"Stuff the yard is going to throw away. They just put it all in a pile and toss it out. Like this paint," Joe said pointing to the large buckets. "Some guy had the paint department do a color match, but they got it wrong. They had to make more, and this gets tossed out."

"So anyone can just take what they want from the pile?" I asked.

"Yeah, but most of us rent our houses, so Mike's the only one who really takes anything. He's been building something in the break room too. He takes wood from the pile, and during his breaks he's been sawing and sanding. I just figured out that it's a coatrack. It's almost done, and, I swear, he could sell that thing for a lot of money. It looks like some expensive thing you'd buy from one of them fancy stores."

"He made it by himself?" I asked, amazed.

"Sure did. And with all free stuff, too."

"I didn't know he knew how to work with wood."

"It might not be proper for me to say this," Joe said, looking at the floor, "but Mike's a decent guy. I know you guys are going through some stress. I saw the story on the news. At first I was real shocked cuz it's not often ya know the guys they talk about on the news. But the next morning when we all got to work, Mike went around and apologized to all of us for what he done. Then we keep hearing him apologize to the customers he runs into that he knew from before. We can tell Mike's one of those guys who just got off track. He won't be working in the yard long. He'll land on his feet. Decent guys always do."

"I hope you're right," I whispered.

"I've got two more sacks in my truck," Joe said as he ran outside. Less than a minute later, he walked back in the front door. "There were a bunch of coloring books that got ripped on the cover," he said handing the kids a large sack, "and some toys that got dropped off a fork lift. They work fine, but the boxes got smashed up so we can't sell them. He told me to tell you he only paid for one thing."

"What is that?" I asked.

"This." Joe reached into his last sack and handed me an ice-cold, twenty-ounce bottle of Cherry Coke.

I knew it sounded childish to shriek gleefully, but I couldn't have been happier.

MIKE'S JOURNAL
12/2/2004

I had a conversation with Sharla at the beginning of this and I told her everything that I had ever held back from her—things from junior high until now. I strongly felt the temptation to hold back and try to make myself look as good as I could, but I was too far gone to do that. So I told her everything I could possibly think of, and all hope of her ever liking me again died. It was a horrifying experience. I cannot think of anything more painstakingly terrible. For both of us.

The look of hurt on her face will never cease to haunt me.

I hope it was the right thing to do. I know it didn't bring us closer, but it gave her all the information.

Last night I had a dream that I died. I have heard that you cannot dream of your own death, but you can.

BLEED MY OWN BLOOD

I was standing in my boys' bedroom putting away their laundry while the animated sound of the children playing in the backyard bounced through the window and danced around the room. I could hear their cheery play at the edges of my thoughts, and it felt like salt in a wound. My mind was occupied with sorrow. I was silently screaming that nothing was fair. I had married an upstanding, moral man whose family I was intimately familiar with. I had supported him in every venture; I kept a clean house and never complained about anything. I had four babies and exhausted myself daily seeing to their needs. And I did it all gladly because I wanted a wonderful marriage. I wanted a happy home. I didn't get what I wanted.

As I tossed Drake's socks into his top drawer, Mike walked into the room and asked me what I wanted for dinner. It was too much. I lost it.

"It doesn't matter what I want!" I turned and screamed at him. "I don't get what I want!" Dropping the rest of the laundry to the ground, I attacked. I rained punches onto his chest, screaming and yelling. I wanted him to feel my pain. I wanted him to hear my anger. Heedless of where the punches were landing, I relentlessly attacked him with a consuming violence that surprised even me. I expected him to step away or tell me to calm down, but he didn't. So I just kept punching, hitting, and screaming.

Finally the anger was released, and I was spent. The sides of my hands were throbbing from the relentless pounding, and I was out of breath. My throat was sore, and I felt like a balloon that had lost all of its air. I raised my eyes and was horrified at what I saw. Mike's face was covered in blood that dripped from his nose and was smeared across his cheeks. Red drops had splattered onto his shirt, and, horrified, I noticed blood on my palms, wrists, and smudged across my fingers.

I shook my head knowing I could not have caused this mess. I am so much smaller than Mike; I never thought I could really hurt him. But the blood was on my hands.

I opened my mouth to apologize, but the words stuck in my throat. I felt terrible about what I had done, but I just couldn't bring myself to offer an apology to the man who had wounded me so deeply. In a moment of pure genius born out of years of knowing and understanding me, Mike wiped his nose with his fingers, stared at the blood, and quoted Ben Stiller from the movie *Dodgeball*, "Nobody makes me bleed my own blood. Nobody."

Mike's humor has always been one of the strengths of our marriage. He can make me laugh at completely inappropriate times like sad movies or church services or hospital visits. He makes me laugh when I want to be mad.

I was helpless against his humor, and I laughed. It was funny. Not what had happened, but how he reacted to what happened. And the movie *Dodgeball*. That was funny, too.

Mike's remorse was evident, and his patience as I processed through the spectrum of emotions was remarkable. But I didn't care. When Christmas drew near, I wrapped up my wedding ring and gave it away in a white elephant exchange.

MIKE'S JOURNAL
12/6/2004

I had another dream that I died. I looked at my lifeless body and felt sorry at the hollowness that pain had carved into my soul. Then God showed up. He picked my dead body up and carried it on His back. He spoke softly, but the words thundered. "I have you," He said.

And the hollowness was not completely empty.

JAIL

"I've been discussing my options with my lawyer," Mike told me after we put the kids to bed. "And I think that Monday morning I will go to the police department and turn myself in."

"What will happen when you do that?" I shook as I asked the question.

"As far as I understand, the officer on duty will listen to my confession. Then they will arrest me and I will go to jail. Then someone, hopefully you, will bail me out so I don't have to stay there."

"Why wouldn't I leave you there?"

"There is no good reason not to."

My phone rang Monday afternoon and my hand shook so much I dropped the phone as I tried to answer it. "I'm your husband's lawyer," a brusque voice said. "I'm going to give you an address and you need to write it down. Then you need to grab a friend and go to the address I give you."

I stepped away from the game of memory I was playing with the kids, and my mind raced trying to make sense out of the orders I was being given. "Why? What is this address for?"

"So you can get a bail bond and get your husband out of jail."

"Is he in jail?" I asked, not recognizing my own voice. The last time I had talked to Mike was when he was leaving to turn himself in at the police station. I suspected a call like this one was likely, but the reality of it was still shocking.

"He's in jail, and you need to get him out. Go to the address I gave you and take your driver's license."

"What if I don't want to get him out of jail? Can't he stay there?"

"Get him out. Leave now. Don't go alone."

The lawyer had hung up, but I kept the phone to my ear for a long time afterward just hoping further clarification was still coming.

Finally, I put down the phone and took some deep breaths. I went into the garage so the kids wouldn't hear or see the uncontrollable sobs that racked my body. I walked to the stack of paint cans sitting haphazardly in the corner and organized them alphabetically by their color name. Then I wondered why I was doing that.

"Mommy, you have a fever," Makenna said when I walked back inside.

"Why do you say that?"

"Your face is super-duper red."

"I think you are right," I told her. "But don't you go worrying about the paint. I totally solved that disorganized mess."

"What?"

"Nothing." I sighed and kissed the satiny top of her head. "I'm going to call Grandma and see if she can come babysit while I have a fever."

"Yeah! Grandma always rubs my feet and my back!"

When I knew my mom was en route to my house, I picked up my phone and dialed one of the youth leaders I still talked to. "Cindy?" I said when she answered. "Will you run an errand with me?"

"Who wrote this?" Cindy asked squinting at the scrap of paper and turning it in her hand.

"I did. I was shaking."

"Well, I'm not familiar with this part of town, but I think you are going to turn right in about four blocks. And it wouldn't be a terrible idea to lock the doors."

Almost every window in the neighborhood was blacked out, and most of the front porches were separating themselves from their house. Nobody was walking alone, but, rather, in groups of intimidating people who had not been taught that staring was rude.

"I didn't even know Des Moines had neighborhoods like this one," I said as I pushed a button and heard the reassuring click of the locks.

"I think that is it," Cindy said, pointing to a dilapidated structure with a small parking lot in front. I nodded when I saw the sign in the window that said Bail Bonds, and I parked my car as near the front door as possible without driving right through it.

When I first walked in, I couldn't see anything. Then, after my eyes adjusted, I wished I couldn't see anything. The dim light dangling from the ceiling was so ineffective it took awhile for me to realize there was a desk in the corner and a man sitting in a folding chair.

"You looking for me?" his deep, coarse voice asked.

"I don't know," I whispered. Clearing my throat I spoke again, this time louder. "My husband is in jail. I need to get him out."

"Then you are looking for me. Sit down."

Cindy and I looked skeptically at the couch. After hesitating, we cautiously sat on the soiled cushions. Then the man in the folding chair asked me a lot of questions and did a lot of typing on his keyboard.

"Do you have a bathroom?" I asked after he had asked me so many questions my tongue was sticking to the top of my mouth.

"Down the hall," he said. "This will be printed when you're done and you can be on your way."

There was only one door in the hallway, but it was smaller than a real door. I am short, and I would have had to duck to enter. I looked around for another door, but couldn't find one. Cautiously, I opened the small door and peeked inside. Scores of roaches skittered for cover when the beam of light penetrated the dark room, and the water dripping from the faucet was a horrid shade of brown. The toilet was filthy, and there was a putrid liquid all over the floor. I could almost smell the bacteria multiplying in the cesspool at my feet. I immediately decided that I would gladly pee in my pants if it meant I did not have to enter that room. I shut the door as quickly as my arm would move and ran to find Cindy.

"Here," the folding-chair man said as he handed me a stack of papers.

"What is this?" I asked.

"It's what you came here for," he answered, rolling his eyes.

"What do I do with it?"

"Just keep it for your records. I already called and got your husband out. He will meet you outside the jail."

"Okay," I said over my shoulder as Cindy and I rushed outside. We heaved ourselves into the car and locked the doors. I started the car but let it idle while I closed my eyes and rested my head on the back of the seat.

I knew that any normal person in my situation would feel angry, maybe even furious, at being placed in such a bizarre situation. I understood that crying would be a perfectly acceptable reaction. I didn't understand, though, why I felt like laughing. I shut my eyes tighter, telling myself sternly not to laugh. That would not make sense. But I kept picturing Cindy and me, two sheltered, naive ladies from the nice side of town, navigating these shady streets, hesitating to sit on a dirty couch, and trying to pretend that we knew what we were doing. I couldn't help it; it struck me as hilarious.

"You know," Cindy said, "when you asked if I wanted to go on an errand with you? I expected Target." And that did it. I allowed myself a small giggle, but was soon consumed by uncontrollable laughter.

"This isn't part of your normal chores?" I asked, doubled up.

"Usually not jail either," she said with a laugh.

"Do you even know where jail is?" I managed to squeak out.

"No!" she wailed, wiping tears from her cheeks. "I was waiting for my pastor's wife to show me."

After we finally located the jail, we found Mike standing on the sidewalk. When I saw him, all the laughter disappeared and fury rippled through me. My hands shook on the steering wheel, and I could barely manage to work the brake in order to stop the car on the side of the street. Cindy slipped to the backseat so Mike could sit in the passenger seat. When he sat down, he whispered a tortured apology and then sat in silence as tears ran down his face.

After we dropped Cindy off at her house, Mike and I drove to the lawyer's office. I had not accompanied him during his prior visits, and I expected plush carpet, a mahogany desk, and bookshelves filled with thick tomes, but we walked into an office with stained carpet, a rickety desk, and two cheap chairs, in which we sat.

"Welcome," a skinny man sitting at the desk said while flipping through a stack of papers. I thought he was the lawyer's aide until he said, "I'll tell you what will happen next, then you'll pay me, and then we can all go home."

"Thank you," Mike said, mostly because there was nothing else to say.

"So, the charge they're going with is sexual exploitation by a counselor—a class D felony. I've already submitted a not-guilty plea, so now they will counter. We might be able to counter back and forth until we come to a compromise. If not, this will go to trial."

"Wait," Mike interrupted. "Why are we pleading not guilty? I am guilty."

"You turned yourself in at a police station and confessed to your pastor. So unless you want to recant the confession you made to your pastor, which I highly recommend, we aren't saying you didn't do something you consider to be morally wrong. We are pleading not guilty to the level of charges. We are saying you are not guilty of a class D felony."

"But, wouldn't I still plead guilty?"

"No. That's not the way this works."

"I just want to make sure I do the right thing," Mike said, rubbing his hand down his face.

"Well, you should have thought of that a year ago. Now that you are in this mess you need to stop thinking about yourself and start thinking about your family. If you accept a felony verdict, you will most likely go to prison. Then what will happen to your family? Who will buy food for your little boys to eat? You're going to send your wife to work? Then who will babysit? Who will pay for daycare? See what I'm saying? You need to stay out of prison. Don't worry about escaping penalty. Staying out of prison will actually be harder on you. You have to find a better job, which will be hard now with your record. Also, this is a high-profile case. Everyone will recognize you from the evening news. Who will hire you after that? Will you have any friends left?

"If you go to prison you'll be one of the most honest men in there. You'll feel pretty good about yourself compared to everyone else. But, out here, you'll have to live with rejection; you'll have to deal with people's anger; you'll have to watch your family suffer while you work day and night and you still might not make it. It's the harder road, so don't worry about doing the right thing. The right thing is to keep your wife home raising your kids. If you go to prison, your family will suffer much more than you will. Believe me."

"Oh. Okay," Mike mumbled. "So what now?"

"Now you can pay me."

DAY OUT

In spite of the trauma I was plowing through, the calendar marched forward and the most magical time of the year drew near. For the first time in my life, the jingling of bells and lighting of trees made me feel like an outsider. I usually love the first snow, the holiday songs, sugar cookies, apple cider, wrapping gifts, all of it. I usually look forward to Christmas more than an adult should. But my world had gone down in flames, and the ashes that were left just couldn't muster up any jolly holiday spirit.

The cheerful music thoroughly depressed me, and the thought of dragging out the tree and decorations overwhelmed me completely. I couldn't bring myself to face all the memories of Christmases past, so the tree stayed in the attic, and the house remained tree free.

"Why don't you let me take care of the kids today and you can get out of the house?" Mike suggested one Saturday when I groggily walked into the kitchen. The three older kids were just finishing their breakfast, and Emery was arranging pieces of fruit into a rainbow on her plate. On his days off from the lumberyard, Mike would let me sleep late as he got the kids ready for the day.

"Are you sure?"

"Absolutely. I've got a lot of fun things planned, and I've already got supper figured out. I think you could use some time to yourself."

I hurriedly brushed my teeth and was half way into my coat when a thought struck me. "Do you ever see people you know from church while you are working?"

"Sometimes."

"Is that awkward?"

"Yeah. I always apologize when I see someone for the first time. Sometimes it's just awkward. Sometimes they actually hug me. Sometimes they just listen and then walk away. One time someone that I recognized but couldn't quite remember got really mad and started yelling at me. It caused a huge scene. A manager from another department had to come settle him down. Why do you ask?"

"Joe said something about it when he was at our house. I've been meaning to ask about it, but I kept forgetting. I think it's good that you do that."

"Thanks. I'm not doing it to be good. It just needs to happen."

The first place I went was the library. I loved the library. The instant I opened the front door I felt safe knowing that in this serene refuge I would not overhear a conversation about my husband or me. I walked around aimlessly, enjoying the peace and quiet. The cozy silence folded around me like a blanket and made my eyes fill with unexpected tears.

I read a few chapters out of different books but couldn't focus long enough to read anything specific. I believe I fell asleep at one point. I stayed longer than somebody no longer in school usually stays at a library.

I met my mom for lunch and insisted we eat Mexican because everybody spoke Spanish. I couldn't tell if they were talking about me. She took me to the mall and bought me some new clothes and treated me to a pedicure.

When I opened my front door at the end of the day, I gasped in shock. The Christmas tree was decorated, the stockings were hung, and the scent of apple cider filled the house.

"You're just in time to frost the cookies." Mike smiled.

"That's my favorite part," I whispered, stunned.

"I know." He walked to where I stood frozen in the doorway and took the sacks out of my hands. "I know you felt overwhelmed by Christmas, so I wanted to have it done by the time you got home today. All the decorations are out, the boxes are back in storage, and we even vacuumed. The kids had a great time helping out, but we saved the frosting until you got home."

I smiled. I've always hated making cookies. It is so tedious. I don't mind mixing all the ingredients together, but I hate forming each cookie, baking them, removing them, and filling another cookie sheet to repeat the whole process. But frosting sugar cookies at Christmastime is different. It's magical.

"Mike," I called to him as he was walking back into the kitchen.

"Yeah?" he turned.

"Thank you."

His eyes twinkled, and he nodded silently before turning back to the kitchen.

MIKE'S JOURNAL
12/9/2004

I can't believe it. Sharla kissed me today. It was so brief I almost thought I had imagined it. But it happened. It was perfect.

I could live on that for the rest of my life.

CHRISTMAS MONEY

As Christmas Day drew near, it was obvious that there was no money for gifts. I kept wishing things would change. I even bought a lottery ticket for the first time in my life although I knew there was almost no chance of winning. I just couldn't bear to tell my children that there would be no gifts under the tree. As much as I tried to avoid it, I eventually had to face reality.

"There is something we need to talk about," I said as I gathered the kids at the kitchen table. Makenna sat still, her large eyes focused on me, while Drake turned sideways in his chair and poked Josiah in the ribs with his big toe. "Drake, don't bother your brother."

"That was on an accident," he said, turning his body to face forward.

"No it wasn't, but that is not what I want to talk about. I need to tell you guys something, and I'm sorry, but it's not happy news."

"What's wrong, Mommy?" Makenna asked.

"Well, Christmas is coming, and we always have a lot of fun during this time of the year, but it's going to be different this time. We are still going to have a great time and make cookies and watch our favorite movies, but when we wake up on Christmas morning we won't have any gifts to open."

"Is it because I poked 'Siah?" Drake asked. "I sorry."

"No, it isn't because of anything you guys did. You have been very good all year and deserve lots and lots of gifts. But, the thing is, sometimes you just don't get what you deserve. Since Daddy is working at the lumberyard, we don't have enough money for gifts this year. If there were any way I could find extra money and buy you guys all your favorite things, I would do it. But it just won't work that way this time."

"What about all the money you made with our computer?" Josiah asked.

"We've already sold everything we can think to sell. Daddy even sold his fishing stuff, and I never thought he would do that. I talked Daddy into selling my hand mixer and my can opener. And we used the money already to pay for things like food and heat."

"We can sell some of my toys," Makenna offered.

Their pouty faces almost broke my heart, and I funneled the disappointment into fury toward Mike. This was all his fault. If he hadn't ruined our lives, I would be out buying Christmas presents right now. I had to endure this because of his selfishness and stupidity, and at that moment I was exceedingly happy that he was working a double shift in the freezing weather.

"Is Christmas canceled?" Josiah asked.

"No, it isn't. In fact, we will still get up on Christmas morning and have Swedish pancakes, like usual. We will still do all of our favorite things. We will go sledding and make hot chocolate. We will watch Christmas movies, and we will be together. And you will still get gifts from your grandparents."

"It will be okay, Mommy." Drake shrugged. "Maybe we can just find stuff for each other and smash it up."

"You mean *wrap* it up," Makenna corrected.

"Smashing is funner," Drake mumbled and Josiah giggled.

"Hugs will make me feel special for Chrissymas!" Emery said, and we laughed at her pronunciation.

"Remember how Daddy made you that coatrack with the pretty knobs so we could hang our jackets and backpacks on it?" Makenna asked.

"Yes," I answered.

"Was that his Christmas to you?"

"No. He just did that to be nice and because I was tired of your jackets and backpacks on the floor all the time. But we could make things for each other. That's a good idea."

"Could we pray for presents?" Makenna asked.

"You can certainly pray, Makenna. This year we will just focus on the real meaning of Christmas instead of the gifts, okay?"

"Jesus is the real meaning," Josiah announced.

"That's right," I said. "And Jesus is the best gift I've ever gotten." Tears flooded my eyes and my throat tightened as I thought about Jesus and how I had depended on Him. I knew I couldn't make one good decision without Him, and His goodness toward me left me undone.

"Are you okay, Mommy?" Josiah asked.

"Yes." I cleared my throat. "I just love Jesus very much."

"Jesus gives all the children hugs," Emery said.

"He does?" Drake asked.

"It's in my Bible," Emery explained as she fiddled with her hair.

"Is there something in your hair, Emery?" I asked.

"Peanut butter is making it sticky," she said.

"Did I give you guys baths this morning?" I asked, suddenly wondering when their last bath had been.

"Daddy did it," Drake said.

"He did?"

"You fell asleep, and Daddy told Makenna to help Emery. But me and Josiah take showers all by ourselves like men."

"What else did Daddy do?"

"He told us a really long story."

"Really?"

"He said he would be at work when we went to bed, so he told us our story this morning. And he said it was backward day because he prayed with us in the morning instead of at night."

"How often does he do that?" I asked.

"He prays with us every day," Makenna answered. "Sometimes at morning and sometimes at night. Sometimes he calls us on the phone and says our prayers while he is eating his supper at work. He eats his supper at our bedtime."

"I didn't know that," I whispered, mostly to myself.

Emery was standing up in her chair, so I told her to sit down and surrounded her with paper and crayons.

"Makenna, will you keep an eye on Emery while I take a quick shower?"

"Sure, and I will make her pray with me so Jesus will send us presents."

"Well, you can pray, but don't expect God to send you presents just because you asked for them." I thought about the balance of our bank account and wondered if I was setting her up for disappointment by encouraging her to pray. I wondered if I should just tell her there was no chance of any gifts, but the hope in her eyes broke my heart, and I couldn't do it.

"What do you want, Josiah?" I responded to his incessant tugging on my hand.

"Follow me," he whispered.

I followed him as he snuck to the bedroom the boys shared. He looked around to make sure we were not being observed and opened the closet door.

"This is Drake's favorite car," he said waving a Hot Wheels car a couple inches in front of my eyes. "He likes it 'cuz it's the fastest car. I can give it to Drake for Christmas."

"You mean wrap up something he already has and give it to him on Christmas morning?"

"Yeah." His big blue eyes twinkled with the brilliance of his plan.

"Won't Drake look for the car before that?"

"Yeah!" He nodded, index finger raised, and explained, "Drake will be sad 'cuz the car is lost, but then he will be so happy when he opens it and can play with it again."

"You truly are a little genius." I laughed and kissed the top of his fuzzy head. "Go for it, buddy. I think that is a great idea."

As I walked toward my bathroom I wondered how in the world God had seen fit to bless me with such incredible children. I had long ago mastered the two-minute shower, so, moments later, I returned to find the children dancing around the living room.

"Mommy, it worked!" Makenna shouted. She danced over to me, waving some paper in the air.

"What worked?"

"Look!" She placed the paper in my hand, and I stared at it, speechless.

"Where did you get this?" I whispered.

"When you were in the bathroom, someone knocked on the door. When I opened it, a lady or an angel was there and said to take this and buy Christmas presents. She said God told her to give it to us. How much money is it?"

"It's a hundred dollar bill."

And then I cried.

MIKE'S JOURNAL
12/17/2004

Validate. Validate. Validate more.

I've talked to Tricia many times about how to respond to Sharla, and she advised me to validate her feelings every time we talk. But the accusations she levels at me are relentless—some even untrue. I am so tempted to defend myself. I want to correct the accusations that aren't true and explain the ones that are.

I did last night. I spoke the rebuttal pent up inside my chest. I spoke it alone in a room so that I could hear the words and she wouldn't have to. Even to me they sounded useless.

Sometimes I feel like I am just her dartboard.

I want to matter, heal, move forward.

I feel meaningless, but I validate her feelings so that she will know she matters so very much.

Even if I am only here to validate her, I am still here.

CHRISTMAS MIRACLE

"I just got the kids to sleep," I told Mike as he stomped through the door, ushering in a cold gust of wind. His stocking hat was frozen to his hair and ice fell from his gloves as he removed them. He kicked off his wet boots, and I inhaled the scent of snow and lumber as I grabbed his stiff and frozen coat and hung it up. "I told you I could pick you up so you wouldn't have to ride your bike home in this weather," I said as I handed him a towel.

"I know," he said, rubbing his face dry with the towel. "But I didn't want you to bring the kids out on a day like this."

"How was work?"

"Christmas Eve in a lumberyard goes by very slowly. Thanks for the hot chocolate. I held onto the thermos to keep my hands warm as much as I could." Mike used his fingers to knock the rest of the snow and ice out of his hair as I grabbed his elbow and pulled him to the corner of the kitchen.

"You won't believe what has happened while you have been at work. You know how we planned to wrap the gifts we bought with that one hundred dollars someone gave us?"

"Yeah." Mike scrunched his forehead, expecting bad news.

"Well, we might be up a long time. People have been leaving gifts for the kids by our front door all evening. I kept hearing quiet knocking sounds on the front door, and when I'd open it, there would be a stack of presents!" I pulled a blanket off the pile of gifts and laughed at Mike's shocked expression.

"I can't believe it," he whispered.

"I know. I can't either. It was really hard to get them all inside without the kids seeing what they were. I had to tell them to watch Christmas movies and not try to peek at what was happening. I could barely get them to sleep, they were so excited."

"We didn't even buy this many gifts during the best of times."

"I know. It's a Christmas miracle."

"We'd better get wrapping. This will take hours."

I felt dazed as I hauled out the wrapping paper, tape, and scissors. With Christmas music playing on the iPod, we got to work.

"We are setting ourselves up for a disappointment next year. The kids will be expecting a mountain of gifts every Christmas from now on," Mike said as he grabbed the final gift and tried to find a space for it near the tree.

"Well, I say we just enjoy this year and worry about next year later."

"Agreed. It's a miracle, and it's meant to be enjoyed. So," he said with a mischievous grin, "what would you say to taking a walk?"

"Right now?"

"Yep."

"But, it's a blizzard! And it's midnight!"

"So, it sounds fun?"

"In a blizzard? What about the kids?"

"They are sound asleep, and we will only go a few houses down. We'll take the monitor."

I tried but could not think of an appropriate response.

"Come on," he said after I stared blankly at him for several moments. "The wrapping is done, it's Christmas Eve, we're in the middle of a crisis, we've just experienced a miracle, and it's beautiful outside."

"Okay." I laughed.

Mike just threw on some tennis shoes, but I wrapped myself in my oversized coat, boots, mittens, and a scarf before heading into the knee-deep snow.

"It's a good thing you came home when you did," I told Mike. "Your bike would never make it through snow like this."

"It's so bright out," Mike said. "Everything looks clean, and the trees look transplanted from the North Pole."

"Yeah, and it's perfectly quiet. Like the whole city has been sound-proofed." I huffed, already out of breath from walking through snow while dressed as a marshmallow. "The snow creates a soft surface on the ground that acts like a muffler. It absorbs and dissipates the sound waves, so everything seems quiet."

"The world looks brand new," Mike said flinging himself, back side first, into the fresh snow. I joined him, and we slid our arms and legs back and forth.

"If new had a smell, it would smell like snow," I thought out loud. "Um, I can't get up."

"That's because you are wearing the entire outdoor department." Mike laughed as he grabbed my hand and pulled me up.

"Careful! I don't want to step on my snow angel."

"Hey," Mike said after pulling me clear of the snow angel, "let's make four more small ones so the kids can see the whole family in the yard when they wake up in the morning."

"When you talk about making small ones, I assume you mean I should make them since I am the only small one between the two of us?"

"Okay, you make them and I will add the detail. I will give Josiah's a football and Drake's a guitar and stuff like that so everybody will know who is who."

"Good plan," I said already flinging myself down into some fresh snow.

When we were done we stomped back into the house, shivering and laughing. I gathered the wet clothes and threw them all into the dryer as Mike made hot chocolate.

"This looks beautiful," I said as I grabbed the steamy cup. The hot chocolate was topped with marshmallows, drizzled with choco-late sauce, and sprinkled with cinnamon.

"Let's drink it by the front window so we can watch the snow," Mike suggested.

"So," I asked, "Emery's angel is praying, but what is Makenna's doing?"

"Singing," Mike explained, wiping chocolate off his upper lip.

"Oh, I see it now. What is yours doing?"

"He is walking to a cross because he needs help. Also, the cross is made out of lumber, so it kind of fits."

"Did you notice that when everything is totally quiet, you can hear the snowflakes falling?" I asked,

We sipped our drinks in silence just listening as the snow covered our angels.

"What is my angel doing?" I asked, breaking the silence.

"Nothing. I just gave yours a halo because you are perfect just as you are."

His comment took me off guard, and I was tempted to make a nasty retort. I wanted to say, "Then why did you screw up our lives?" or "So perfect isn't good enough for you?" In the end, though, I decided to enjoy the moment and focus on the miracle of Christmas.

Instead, I said, "You know that our angels will all be covered up by morning, don't you?" The snow was already smoothing away most of the angel family.

"I know," Mike said as he drained the last of his hot chocolate. "But they're not gone—they're just tucked in. I will never forget them or this night. This is a perfect Christmas Eve. And I'd like to give you your gift now." He handed me a box wrapped in black roofing paper and sealed with duct tape. When I opened it, a tall statue of a man and a woman embracing fell into my lap.

"Look at the title on the bottom," Mike said.

"*Promise*," I read.

"Yeah. It is titled *Promise*. Now read this." Mike handed me a typed letter. I took a deep breath as my heartbeat increased.

"I found this figurine," the letter began, "and instantly I thought of you and how I wanted to give you a gift like this. I knew I would never be able to, but I bought it anyway. The word *promise* makes me cringe. It brings up feelings of regret and self-disappointment. How can I make a promise that you will believe? How can I even say that word to you? I put the statue in my backpack and thoughts of it gnawed at the back of my brain. Boy, I wanted to give it to you, but I didn't feel worthy or capable of uttering a word like that aloud. It was a term from a different era and a bygone season … just out of grasp.

"Then, one day, you came home when I wasn't expecting you—I had the statue on my desk. I needed to stash it quickly so you wouldn't see it. I grabbed it, but it fell. It landed just right—or wrong—and the man's head came off. I watched it happen in stunned silence, mouth agape. I quickly grabbed both pieces and shoved them into the drawer. Time marched on, and I pulled it out of its hiding place months later. A little superglue, a steady hand, and, minutes later, the head was reattached. Nothing to show for it but a bonk on the head and a line around the neck … promise restored? Now this gift seemed more appropriate."

The words blurred on the page, and I couldn't help sobbing.

"Are you okay?" Mike asked. "Are you upset?" But I couldn't answer. I buried my face into his shoulder and cried. Mike rubbed my back and stroked my hair until my sobs settled down.

"I haven't finished the letter yet," I told him.

"Really? You're already crying and you aren't even through the letter yet?"

"Yep," I said as I dried my cheeks on my sleeve and found the letter.

"Two lives," I read, "dropped to the ground. A promise broken. A guy loses his head and carefully has it supernaturally put back on, and the whole time the promised arms are wrapped around him. A promise restored. Now the sculpture is appropriate. A promise has come back into season. I stand here—one hand grasping your waist and one hand holding yours in awe of the promise you kept and the fact that you haven't left. Merry Christmas."

By the time I was done reading the letter, I was weeping. The statue so perfectly symbolized us—the beauty and the pain, the brokenness, the potential, the hope.

"It's perfect. I love it and always will."

MIKE'S JOURNAL
1/9/2005

It was humbling to be hired by a public relations person who was younger than me, work for a manager who seemed like a kid, and have a job where I replaced a guy who could no longer work because he had brain damage. It feels humiliating to work, at my age, for an hourly wage and clock out and in for lunch. At work an overwhelming depression settled in my soul as I thought of all that I've lost. I whined internally all morning. Then Sharla and Emery came to see me for lunch. I was adding wood to some treated lumber and looked up and saw two pink beacons walking toward me. They stood out so brightly in the overcast day. It was like a ray of sunshine. After lunch I clocked in and changed my perspective. Instead of counting my losses, I began to count my blessings: my job, a lot of alone time at work, time to pray and think. When I started feeling sad, I would just sing: Jesus, lover of my soul; Jesus, I will never let you go.

THE ROAD

My mom had the kids for the day, and I was trying to accomplish all my errands before meeting Mike at a counseling appointment. I had already been to the grocery store and was just leaving the bank after attempting to raise our balance above zero. I checked my rearview mirror so I could back out of my parking space when *Boys of Summer* came on the radio. Instantly, I was sixteen again driving my rusted Monte Carlo. Where did I want to go? To Lori's to watch movies? To the mall?

I just wanted to drive fast and with no destination in mind. I cranked the volume and rolled the windows all the way down as I drove down the entrance ramp to the interstate. Icy wind whipped across my face and numbed my cheeks. The broken yellow lines on the pavement blurred as I accelerated well beyond the posted speed limit, and, soon, the city was behind me – a memory if I chose so. I felt the road calling me on, faster and faster. The song was over, but Don Henley's voice filled my head, "Don't look back. You can never look back. I thought I knew what love was, what did I know? Those days are gone forever, I should just let them go…"

I don't know how many songs played before I lost my radio signal and began scanning through stations to find another one. I stopped when I heard Bruce Springsteen and sang *Born in the USA* with The Boss. I flung my hand out the window so I could feel the freezing wind on my fingers, wrist, and palm. I cupped my hand, and the wind filled it, numbed it.

I drove faster and faster until I was pushing the limits of my mini-van, and the further I drove, the more free I felt. Every exit sign I passed pushed me further away from the trouble I wanted to leave behind. I relaxed as I saw more and more road in my rearview mirror.

I stopped for gas in a town so small it didn't own a stoplight and wondered what life would be like in such a rural place. It might be nice to be so hidden from society. Or nosey neighbors might absorb each other's privacy until such a concept was merely a faint sugges-tion. I drove on.

At some point I turned off the interstate and down a gravel road. I passed a barn, but there were no horses or cows in sight. Fields of alter-nating beige and black stripes stretched straight until they met the sky. Straggling trees grew thicker as the path I drove narrowed, and the over-growth of nature blocked out the sun, covering the gravel like a cave.

Music blaring, I glanced at the groceries on the seat beside me, and I hated them. They tied me to a responsibility that was crush-ing me and a life that no longer felt like mine. I grabbed a bottle of ketchup and threw it out the window. It hit a tree and exploded, red chaos covering the tree trunk, dripping down the bark. Smiling, I tossed an egg out the window. It landed in tall grass, and I couldn't see the mess it made. I grabbed the rest of the eggs, one after the other, and lobbed them at fences and branches, and I laughed when they hit their mark and popped. Next was a bag of flour. I threw it at a fence post, but it was heavy and burst against a nearby tree trunk instead. A cloud of white dust obscured the road in my rearview mir-ror. Laughing, I grabbed the last item – a gallon of milk. It took two hands to lob it out the window, and I laughed as it broke, drenching grass and leaves and tree bark in a white coat.

I suddenly realized that, although I had slowed considerably, I was going much too fast for the prevalent potholes and the trees that were crowding the increasingly narrow route. Branches scraped my windows as I barreled my car between the trees, and, when I slammed on the brake, my car slid, narrowly missing a wide trunk. Heart racing from the near miss, I stared at the tree no more than two inches away from my hood.

For the first time in hours, I looked around. I was lost. I suspected that I wasn't on a road at all. After attempting to reverse several times, I tried to drive forward but stopped when I heard the underbelly scrape against the gravel. Arms covering my beige, leather steering wheel, I pressed my forehead against my wrists and cried until the neck of my sweatshirt was soaked. I screamed and yelled, as if Mike was in the seat next to me, able to hear my insults. I wailed and asked God how He could let my life become so hopeless. I shouted to sixteen-year-old me, bright-eyed and optimistic. I warned her against the blazon happiness she displayed, and I wanted to slap her smiling face.

Spent, I learned my head against the window and fell asleep. The daylight was seeping from the sky when a thumping near my head awakened me. I blinked as I tried to remember where I was. The thumping repeated, more insistent, and I jumped so hard I jammed my knee against the dashboard when I saw a man in a cowboy hat standing beside my door, knocking on the window. Although his face didn't reveal an age, the hair escaping from his hat was gray, and when he rested his hand on the hood of my car, I could tell he was in his twilight years. His flannel jacket looked older than me.

"Do you know you're on private property?" he asked when I rolled the glass down.

"Sorry," I shrugged, still groggy. "I'm lost."

"I thought as much," he said. "I don't get a lot of minivans down here."

"Yeah, I was acting like I was driving a Monte Carlo."

"Huh?" he stared at me, confused.

"Nothing."

"I can get your car out of the hole you're in if ya want to step out for a minute."

I stood helplessly in the grass as he did some magic involving a chain and a big truck.

"Thanks so much," I told him when he was finished rescuing me.

"No problem. Added a little excitement to my day is all."

"Well," I tried to recover, "at least I missed your tree. I almost ran right into it."

"Looks like ya had a little spill too," he said and gestured toward the road I had baptized in eggs, flour, and milk. The ketchup was out of sight, but I could picture it covering a tree trunk.

"Oh," I said, grimacing, "sorry about that. My life is a little messed up right now."

"Yeah, I thought so," he scratched his forehead with his thumb, raising his hat up and then back down several times.

I felt terrible and wondered how to explain myself, but when he smiled down at me I didn't see any judgment in his expression.

"My life has gotten pretty messed up a time or two," he said softly.

"What did you do? How did you handle it?"

"I woke up in the morning, did what needed done, and woke up the next morning. Then I repeated that schedule until things started making more sense, and eventually they kinda did."

"Well, I don't know what kind of mess you were in, but I'm in a marriage mess."

He laughed out his nose without taking his eyes off of the past he seemed to be looking at and said, "That's the only kind of mess there really is. Everything else is small stuff."

"Was it bad?"

"It was bad." He tore his eyes from his memories and glanced at me. After a moment of hesitation, he took a deep breath and continued. "She wanted babies so bad it was all she could think of. She got angry and took it out on me. One day she just ran off. Up and left with a traveling sales man."

"I'm sorry. Did you ever hear from her again?"

"She came back after about a year. She walked through the front door with her head hung down, so skinny – like she hadn't had a meal since she left. I thought I was looking at a ghost."

"Did you let her stay?"

197

"Yep."

"Do you love her?"

"I love that woman so much it hurts. I tell her every week when I visit her grave."

I looked up at him, wondering if I heard his words correctly. He laughed and laid a thick hand on my shoulder. "You kids," he said. "You think your whole life rests on one decision. Well, life is messier than that. What if I couldn't forgive the woman I loved? In my opinion, that says more about me than about her.

"Welp," he sighed, "she got breast cancer a few years back. She was real sick, and then she was gone. What if I had let my pride turn her out that day she walked back through my door? I wouldn't have had all that extra time with her. I'd be the one who lost."

"I missed our counseling appointment," I confessed. "I was supposed to meet my husband this morning. It would be hard to explain that."

"Probably not as hard as ya think."

"Do you want me to pay for the damages I caused?" I asked, sorry about the mess I had made on his land.

"I surely do not." He opened the front door so I could get back into the van. "Follow this gravel road for about five miles. Then you'll get to a T intersection. A right turn will take you away, and a left turn will take you back to Iowa."

He laughed when I looked at him surprised. "I don't get a lot of cars down here," he said, "but I still know an Iowa license plate when I see one."

I drove the way he told me to, and when I came to the T intersection, I stopped and turned off my car. I thought it over for a long time, and then I laughed. The symbolism hit me so hard, I couldn't help but find it funny.

I had expected my life to be pleasant, like a fun road trip, but my peaceful expectations twisted on me. The road I started out on had become hard—nearly impossible. Sometimes I didn't know my way, and I felt stuck. I found myself wishing for my old life back – wishing

I could get into a car, play music from the 80's, and drive myself to a place and time that felt familiar.

But that old road was gone, vanished into the past. It wasn't my desire or my choice that made it disappear, but I was still trying to travel down a path that no longer existed. I was on a new journey whether I wanted to be or not.

And my new journey was scary and more difficult than I wanted it to be. It hurt. But one thing was for sure: it would take me somewhere. If I chose my steps carefully, maybe it would take me somewhere good, somewhere I would want to arrive at. Maybe it was perfect for me.

Perfect for me does not mean the same thing as easy for me; it simply means that it is as it should be. My path was perfect for me. As much as I resisted believing it, I knew it was true.

I was not alone though. I felt the ever-present tether tighten, and I knew God had the other end wrapped around His wrist as He walked with me, step for step. That tether was the only thing that was certain. That, and four chubby-cheeked, needy, cuddly towheads.

The path loomed before me, treacherous and demanding. It would require intense work, and it would strip me of all that I clung to. But I was tethered.

I turned left.

MIKE'S JOURNAL
1/25/2005

It was my birthday, and for the first time since we were married, Sharla didn't celebrate it. I didn't expect her to since my very touch repulses her. Even if I just bump into her arm, she recoils. Anytime I see any spark of passion, it is immediately gone. She shuts down totally.

This has been a hard struggle for me because I feel like I'm dying inside. I have this strong desire for her touch that is screaming inside of me. But there is no hope of getting that need met.

I want to be better than I am. I want to be able to handle this, but it is impossible. So many inadequacies all at once.

It would help if she would even just ask how my day was every once in a while.

SNOWBALLS

I opened my freezer one day and was surprised at what I saw.

"Who filled the ice bin with snowballs?"

"They melt when they aren't cold, Mommy," Drake explained.

I sighed. "Yes, I can see how that would happen."

"I made so many snowballs and hid 'em under the droopy tree so 'Siah couldn't find them, but Brinkley, the big, white dog, peed on them. So I told Brinkley to go home and made more and put them in the freezer so Brinkley couldn't find them."

"Mama," Emery said, "the ways of boys are strange. Do not try to mess with it—it only makes it worse." I agreed as I opened a can of Dr. Pepper and drank it warm.

I sat down at the kitchen table and looked around. The boys were working on a puzzle, Makenna was reading a book, Emery ran to her room with a coloring book, and Mike was at work. I watched my children as they did the stuff that fills the days of childhood. Josiah wrestled the last puzzle piece out of Drake's hand and popped it in the hole to complete the puzzle, and Drake threw himself to the ground in protest. I smiled, thinking that I would normally discipline such behavior, but I just didn't have the energy. I was worried about the bills we had no way to pay. I worried that someone might get sick or hurt, and I worried about not having any health insurance. I wondered what would become of my marriage and my future.

I began to feel very overwhelmed and depressed as I wondered why my life was turning out to be a tragedy instead of a fairy tale. My mind was flooded with thoughts that I knew were not healthy, but they just marched across my brain like an unwanted, yet comforting parade. I thought about getting in my bed and sleeping until next month. I thought about turning my kids against their dad by telling them that he had ruined our lives. I thought about using a sharp knife to cut the skin covering my heart to let the pain out.

I was scared. I was terrified. I worried constantly about what people were saying or thinking. I worried about living the rest of my life with somebody I could not forgive. I worried about trying to raise four kids on my own. I worried that if I did forgive my husband, he might stop being sorry for what he had done to me.

MIKE'S JOURNAL
2/12/2005

I realized something—I made my vows not only to Sharla, but to God. They were sacred. Treating something that is sacred as though it is common is pride. I look back in horror and regret at what I have done. Though the consequences seem grim, the act of sin seems so vile and wrong. It is beyond explanation. I am so sorry for what I chose to do. The sin I have committed is so grievous and awful that I cannot conceive how God can forgive me.

If not for the stories in the Bible of Moses, David, Peter, and others, I would believe forgiveness to be out of the question. However, God was even more merciful than Moses when he was dealing with Miriam and Aaron.

Although my sin is always before me, God's truth is lodged in my heart. He accepts the prodigal.

OFF THE GRID

"Whatever happened with that guy, Rob, from therapy?" I asked Mike one day as he was preparing to leave for work and then go to therapy directly after he got off. "The guy that started the same time you did and needed an address. Did he find a place to live?"

"Yeah, his cousin has some property out in the country that has an old Morton Building on it. Rob is living there, but it doesn't have heat or electricity. I'm actually pretty worried about him. He doesn't have any support, and living out there all alone, he gets pretty depressed."

"Are you worried he might try to kill himself?" I asked, handing Mike a sandwich to put into his lunch box.

"Either that or commit another crime. I'm finding out that the system works kind of backward. There are laws that make people feel safe, but those same laws actually make offenders more dangerous. Like Rob. Even though his crime did not involve any minors, he isn't allowed to live within two thousand feet of a school. That sounds good to parents, but if you take into account every school, homeschool, or daycare, he can't find a place in town that he can live. He can't even find a run-down, crappy apartment. He found a house once, but then discovered a home daycare down the block. So, he ended up out in the country all alone. There is no phone and no way for Dan to check in on him regularly. Living in isolation makes him feel worthless, and that worthless feeling makes him feel like he might as well go ahead and reoffend because nobody cares about him anyway.

"This is exactly why a lot of sex offenders end up going into hiding or becoming homeless. They can't find anywhere to live, but if they don't report an address, they will go to jail. So they drop off the grid. They go missing, and that is when they become more dangerous than if they lived in the city where they could be held accountable. They feel hated by society, unlovable, and they are homeless. That kind of stress is a recipe for acting out.

"In my case, it isn't only the threat of prison that makes me want to stay out of trouble. The support I've gotten from you and my family and watching how much suffering my selfish actions caused all of you makes doing the right thing a simple choice. When you don't see how much suffering your actions caused because you are isolated and alone, it is easy to tell yourself that nobody was affected."

"That is a real problem," I said. "I can totally see how Rob would be much more dangerous alone and depressed. I guess I can understand both sides."

"I know," Mike agreed, shrugging into his jacket. "I think I'll drive out this week and see Rob. There is an old fireplace in the junk heap at work, and I'm sure I could fix it. I might take it out to Rob so he can have some heat."

MIKE'S JOURNAL
2/19/2005

I realize that it is of the utmost importance that I respond to Sharla in the way she needs. However, that means I am alone in dealing with the worries that occupy my mind constantly: financial ruin, failure, mortification, loss of all I know, worry, exhaustion. I understand that I have no right to voice those frustrations right now—I brought them upon myself.

I think I have done a fairly good job of interacting with her, but I have blown it at other times and with other people. I snapped at a coworker, I threw a hammer through a piece of drywall in my garage, and, especially, I beat myself up internally quite often.

I just feel so alone.

However, I am confident that God is with me. Therefore, I have all I need for the situation ahead of me. I trust in His promises; they are my armor.

POWER OF LOVE

People had all kinds of names for what my husband was. They said he was a hypocrite. They said he was an abuser. They said he was a reprobate. A lot of people hated him and wished terrible things on him.

I was a bipolar, emotional missile. At moments I would agree with all those people, and I would lash out at him, yelling and screaming. Then there were other moments when I would see his remorse and his efforts to save his family, and I would know there was room for grace, and I believed, maybe just for a moment, that love was stronger than anger.

Love is mysterious. It seems so emotional. We tend to think of it as a fluffy cloud—pretty but insubstantial. Like its sole purpose is to make us feel good and happy. We don't realize that love contains vast power.

We think of anger, vengeance, and hatred as powerful tools, and we wield them proudly. We wave our sharp tools around in a display of control, threatening anyone who does us wrong, and all the while we are slicing our souls. We don't realize that love is the greatest tool of all because it brings life instead of death, and, in the process of using it to cover the sin done against us, we also save ourselves.

I have a neighbor that used to annoy me, and just seeing him walking toward my house would justify a roll of my eyes. This neighbor would steal the sacks of cans I had saved up to redeem for five cents each. Also, he would walk up and down my driveway talking about the oil spots on the concrete and how I should clean them. He made sure to comment when my grass was too long or too weedy or too brown. He made me grind my teeth.

Then I found out he has Asperger's Syndrome. He can't help it. He suffers from a disorder in his mind. I felt like a jerk. I was suddenly patient and caring and actually looked forward to my conversations with him. Now I find him easy to be around, and I don't take his comments personally.

My newfound patience with this neighbor comes from understanding him. Understanding brings grace.

I wanted an explanation for my husband. I wanted to call him something that would help me understand his behavior and why he had hurt me. I wanted to file him into a column that I could live with. My mind obsessed over this puzzle for months before wearing itself completely out and entering a state of shutdown.

So I picked up a paintbrush. People deal with pain in different ways. My way involves a lot of painting the rooms in my house. It probably isn't normal, I know. My therapist didn't suggest it to me. In the process of redecorating our house on a minimal budget, I had found creativity to be energizing and painting to be a peaceful therapy. So I pushed my daughter's furniture away from the walls and began transforming her room into a yellow paradise. I put on some music and let my mind run free. That is when it happened. Clarity.

I'm not one to say that God spoke to me or that I've heard from on high. But something happened. Something I have no label for.

As I painted, I accosted God. "What is it to you?" I asked Him. "Is it hopeless? Is it abuse? Is it immaturity? Is it lack of love? Is it forgivable? What is it to you?" Then, in my head, I heard an answer. I heard it as loud as a train thundering through that little bedroom: To me it is sin.

Sin. A horrible and wretched wrong. A horrible and wretched wrong that can be overcome. A horrible and wretched wrong that can be forgiven. Clarity. I felt like a horse with his blinders just off. But I kept it to myself. What had happened to me in that small bedroom had no label, and I didn't know how to explain it.

MIKE'S JOURNAL
3/11/2005

I chose to sin. I was doing what I wanted without considering the needs of anyone else. I was selfish, but there was something else even darker at the core. I sinned, first, against God. I would like to say it was selfishness, but it was a sin much deeper, much more powerful. I thought I could get away with what God had clearly forbidden. There is only one sin that snubs its nose at God like that: pride. In arrogance, I thought I was above the rules, above getting caught, unstoppable.

I was so wrong.

There is no one greater than the Lord of heaven and earth. His wisdom and power are without comparison throughout all eternity.

I repent of my pride. I understand my place. I cannot even move without God's help. I long for healing.

THE DEAL

D an had subjected Mike to three different polygraphs during the course of their sessions together, and I couldn't have thanked him more. All three polygraphs confirmed that Mike was telling the truth. I was able to meet individually with Dan several times, and I appreciated his direct manner. He told me that he would not hesitate to send Mike directly to jail the moment he felt that Mike was being manipulative or untruthful.

During one of my private sessions, he told me that he had worked with a lot of men in Mike's situation. He told me that usually a man's first story is only a version of the truth. Then his story would change. Then it would change again. After months, the complete truth would be revealed. However, Mike's confession had been complete the first time and had remained unchanged through all of the digging and through three polygraphs. That was rare.

"This is a copy of his assessment," Dan told me. "It takes into account the polygraphs, our sessions, his group performance, as well as the multitude of other tests we have administered. You can read it."

I took the crisp, white paper laced with condemning black words and braced myself against their impact. "It is clear that the client has assumed accountability for the crime for which he is accused. There is no evidence that the client is attempting to minimize his responsibility or to project blame onto his victim. He is highly motivated for treatment and appears capable of working toward change. He is capable of expressing extreme remorse and is motivated to complete his treatment."

"This is good, right?" I asked

"It is as good as I have ever seen, honestly." I had a fleeting thought that Dan must special order his suit coats. He wasn't overweight, but he was very large, and, although I felt his sturdy personality to be comforting, I could understand why Mike felt intimidated by him. I wouldn't want Dan to ever set his mind against me. "I haven't told Mike this, but I believe that he is truly repentant. I wouldn't ever promise anything, but I believe that it is unlikely Mike will do anything like this again in his lifetime."

While I was comforted to hear Dan's thoughts, the suspense of the legal proceedings seemed unendingly slow to me. Every day I felt the instability of our life. Days felt like months as I continuously wondered how I would provide for the kids if Mike ended up in prison. I worried that I would fail. I considered working for minimum wage and leaving the kids with their grandmas, but I knew it wasn't fair to ask anyone to take on the full-time responsibility of four kids. Emery was not yet in school, and transporting the older three to and from school each day as well as helping with their school projects, making lunches, and caring for them after their school day ended, was a lot to juggle. Also, I didn't think I could bear to give up so much time with my children. Even though their constant care was overwhelming, time with them was still the best part of my day.

After many hours of deliberation, I came up with a backup plan. If Mike got sentenced to prison, I would move into a homeless shelter. I did some investigation and found one in Louisiana that accepted workers with children. The parent was required to work for free, but the entire family received meals and a place to sleep. Health concerns were handled at a nearby, low-income hospital, and there was a public school within walking distance. The school was failing in most subjects, but I knew I could work with my kids and teach them what they missed from their classes. It was the only possibility that I could think of that allowed me to provide food and shelter as well as keep us together most of the time. I figured that the kids could help at the shelter, and they might benefit from working to help those stricken with poverty. I didn't want to uproot them and move them far away, but I knew we could do it. I knew I could make the best of it, and we would be okay.

Then our lawyer called us into his office.

"We have a plea deal," he stated bluntly from behind his faux-wood desk. "You agree to three counts of a misdemeanor charge, which is much better than a felony. Then you agree to two years on probation and ten years of registering as a sex offender."

"That's the deal?" I asked.

"That's the deal," he nodded. "No prison. Just probation. With the sex offender registry there are some requirements. You'll have to wear an ankle bracelet that tracks your location for the two years of probation. Any time you go somewhere you shouldn't, your probation officer will know."

"Where am I not allowed to go?" Mike asked.

"You can't leave town unless you get permission first. You can't go into a bar. If you go pick your kids up from school you'll have to let your probation officer know first. Things like that. It's your decision though. We can still take this to trial."

"What would be the benefit of going to trial?" I asked.

"I'm a great lawyer," he said, not bragging, just stating the truth. "I've gotten much worse men out of much worse situations. I'm pretty sure I could get Mike off free and clear. Actually, I could do it pretty easily. No probation. No registry. Nothing."

"So, what would the drawback be?"

"The trial could be a long, drawn-out nightmare for you. Probably would be. My concern about that would be mostly for your kids. They are young, and it would affect them. How are they doing so far?"

"They're great kids." Tears filled my eyes as I thought of their innocent faces. "It has been hard. I'm having a difficult time finding any friends that can still play with them. Even if I suggest that we meet at a park or a movie, most of their friends just can't play."

"Well, unfortunately, if this goes to trail you can expect more of that."

"I'll do whatever you want," Mike told me as we discussed it after the kids went to sleep that night, "but I feel that I should agree to whatever consequences the other lawyer feels to be appropriate. I deserve to pay the price for what I did. I deserve worse than what they are offering, and I can't stand watching the children suffer any more than they already have." So, we agreed to the deal. I was just thankful to put an end to the legal anxiety.

MIKE'S JOURNAL
3/13/2005

I f you believe wrong, you behave wrong, and you will begin to look for other options that seem more satisfying to you than God.

There is a message I have been screaming in my head for the last twenty-six years. The message is that I am not good enough and never will be.

However, I see now that I have the power to change that message. I have to go to the shameful, embarrassing parts of myself, and, instead of having anger and hatred toward that part of me, I can have compassion. There will be no true life for me unless I can show myself compassion without judgment. I will not be whole until I do. And when I show self-compassion, I can change the internal conflict and have hope for a different and whole life.

Amazing.

POLICE

I noticed the police car in the driveway seconds before I heard an insistent knock on the door. Shaking so much I could barely turn the doorknob, I cracked the door open.

"I'm Officer Draper," a uniformed man with a deep voice told me as he flashed his badge. "This is Officer Davorick. Is Mike Hintz at home?"

"No," I tried to say, but mostly formed my mouth into the shape of the word.

"But he does live here?" Officer Draper asked.

"Yes," I managed to say. "He is at work. Is there a problem?"

"No, we are just verifying addresses this afternoon. Since this is our first visit here, can we come in and take a look around?"

"Sure," I said opening the door wider. I stood aside nearly tripping over my own feet to let the two officers inside.

"This is a nice house," Officer Davorick said opening the kitchen cupboards and looking inside.

"Thanks. We've been redecorating," I said, and then I wondered if that sounded like a stupid thing to say. I wondered if I should stand or sit while they invaded my privacy. I opted for nervously alternating between the two.

"I don't see any alcohol in your house," Officer Draper said returning from the basement. "Is there any I missed?"

"No, we don't drink," I answered.

"Well, it's not allowed to be in the house since Mike is on probation. If I drive by later tonight, will I see him here?"

"Yes, unless I kick him out," I joked. And then realized that I shouldn't.

"If he doesn't stay here, he will need to report to his probation officer immediately."

"Don't worry, she'll track him down with that fancy ankle bracelet," I continued to joke and then immediately told myself not to act like an idiot.

"Has he had any problems with the tracker?" Officer Davorick asked.

"Well, he's had to endure the jealousy of all his friends," I said before my brain could stop me. Both officers looked at me sternly and a bit confused, so I continued, finally sounding like a sensible adult, "It started beeping during a movie the other night."

"It will beep if he is out past curfew," Officer Draper told me.

"I know. He is always home by ten, but it was only eight fifteen."

"Did he call in when that happened?"

"Yes."

"Anything else like that?"

"It happened at the grocery store and at church. That doesn't make you popular at church."

"I wouldn't imagine so. Did he call in those times too?"

"Yes."

"Has he done or said anything to concern you?"

"Not besides the obvious reason that you are here in the first place."

"Here's my card. Call if you need anything. We will be stopping by every once in a while just to check up on things."

I closed the door behind them and then ran to the bathroom and threw up.

INTENSIVE

Tricia, whom I talked to almost daily, happened to be a marriage therapist. She was understanding, calm, encouraging, and full of wisdom. I will never be able to thank her enough.

She suggested that Mike and I attend a marriage intensive. The concept is quite unique. You go into a room with four other couples and two counselors. Each couple takes a turn explaining their situation to the group. When I discovered we would need to tell perfect strangers what we were dealing with, I almost refused. There is nothing more frightening than sharing your most painful secrets with a group of people you have never met, and to make matters even worse, I had come down with a case of shingles and had a painful rash on my back.

We were the first to share. That is what you get for sitting next to the counselors.

The first sentence was the hardest. The words practically choked me as they came out. But then the rest of it gushed out like shaken champagne from a newly opened bottle. I actually felt free to be completely honest with this group because they didn't know us and I knew we would never see them again.

"Sharla," the counselor said when I had finished my story, "I've noticed that you seem very uncomfortable. Is it because this is hard to talk about?"

"Oh, no," I answered. "I have rickets."

"Shingles," Mike corrected. "She has shingles."

"Right. Shingles. I can never remember the name of it."

The couple next to us was in bad shape. The husband, whom I will call Dan since I don't remember his name, had been having a succession of affairs since the third month of their marriage. He had acquired two secret children and a disease in the process. The wife, who I will call Diane, was the nastiest person I've ever met. She was crass and loud, and I found it challenging to be around her. I was pretty sure they were doomed.

The couple next to them mistakenly thought they had signed up for a couple's retreat and were looking forward to a nice vacation. I laughed at them.

I will call the next people Mark and Mary. Mary was a sweet woman and had no idea why her husband didn't love her anymore. She guessed maybe it was because she had gained some weight. Mark would neither confirm nor deny the truth of that. Mark didn't speak a word for the next two days. I thought they were doomed.

I will call the next couple Steve and Stacy. Steve was a loud-mouthed alcoholic who refused to give up drinking. He was abusive, demanding, and selfish and had no desire to change. Stacy was a quiet, mousy woman who rarely spoke and mostly nodded. They were doomed.

I left the first session feeling oddly encouraged. Mike had broken down completely during the telling of our story. He begged the counselors to help him and then got onto his knees and apologized over and over while sobbing into my lap.

We agreed to only talk about our problems during the sessions, so in the evenings we could relax. An early spring had arrived in southern Missouri, which was at least twenty degrees warmer than where we lived in Iowa. We had left freezing temperatures that were setting record lows, so although it was still rather chilly, we took a long walk until it was too dark to see. I was struck by the pink and violet blooming all around us contrasting with the new, green grass. The musty smell of foliage soothed my lungs. The call of earth seeped into me and resonated with the earthen blueprint in my soul.

I was the first one in the room the morning of the second day, so I chose a seat far from the counselors hoping to whittle down the chances of being the first to speak. Mary entered the room shortly after me, and I noticed that she had been crying.

"Come sit by me," I called to her.

"Thanks," she said sheepishly as she sat down and took a deep breath.

"Are you okay?"

"I'm just feeling a little hopeless. Mark won't talk about anything, and I feel like we are wasting time being here."

"I'm so sorry." My heart broke for her.

"Are you okay?" she asked, a strange look on her face.

"Yeah, I'm fine," I assured her, feeling a bit guilty about the progress we were making as a couple and Mike's willingness to be open.

"It's just that you keep scratching."

"Oh! That's nothing," I assured her. "I have scurvy."

"Shingles," Mike corrected as he entered the room and handed me a mug of hot tea. "She has shingles."

"That is so hard to remember. *Shingles* doesn't sound like the name of a sickness."

"You should probably remember it though before you send people into a panic," he laughed. "If you're not careful, you'll find yourself in quarantine."

"What kind of tea is this? I love it!"

"Green pomegranate. I knew you'd like it." Mike smiled. "You like fruity teas."

"I do?"

"Yes," he nodded.

"How sweet is that?" Mary sighed. "He knows your drink order."

"Apparently, he knows it better than I do. But, now that I think about it, you're absolutely right. I do like fruity teas. And I really hate most flavors that aren't fruit." I stared at Mike, amazed. "How did you know that about me? I didn't even notice it."

"I know it sounds stupid since we are here because of me, but I pay attention to you. I know you believe I couldn't possibly love you, but I do. Everything you do is important to me; I notice you and I know you. I know you don't like hot chocolate unless it has marshmallows on top. Then you love it. I know you hate the cold weather, but you get excited to put the flannel sheets on the bed. I know that even though fires make your eyes turn red and water, you will sit and watch the flames burn until nothing is left. I know you have a spot just under your left shoulder blade that constantly itches"—he smiled at me— "even when you don't have shingles."

I sat speechless as the counselors entered the room and began the session. They took turns asking us mind-boggling questions, drawing stuff on a dry-erase board, and performing psychological magic that left us sitting, mouths agape, in various stages of revelation about ourselves, our partners, and our situations. I can't even explain what happened. I only know that when I left that room I felt like I could fly if I chose to, and at the same time, I felt like sleeping for a hundred years. I looked at Mike and understood him. I still wanted to throw things at him, but I understood him.

"What would you like to do this evening?" Mike asked after we had eaten that night.

"I think I just want to build a fire and stay in our room." I was exhausted from the mental gymnastics from earlier that day and wanted to give my mind a break. The bed and breakfast we were staying at was cozy and beautiful, and our room had an amazing stone fireplace.

"Are you sure you don't want to go shopping or for a walk or something?" Mike asked as he began stacking logs in the fireplace.

"Yes. I'm exhausted. And my scoliosis is really bothering me."

"Shingles!" He laughed. "Why don't you go take a hot bath while I get this fire going?" he suggested. "You were cold all day in that room, and the hot water will probably help with your headache."

"How did you know I had a headache?" I had not mentioned it, but my head had been throbbing all through dinner.

"Your eyes get a little slanty when you have a headache." He grabbed some twigs and broke them into small pieces for kindling.

"What?" I asked, feeling my eyes with my fingers. "They get slanty?"

"Just a little," he smiled. "I'm sure nobody else noticed."

I made the bath extra hot and bubbly. As the hot water melted away the tension in my neck, I let my mind drift. I thought about how much I missed my kids. I remembered the first date Mike took me on when he gave me the roses in the stream. I thought about how I understood myself more than I had thought possible just yesterday, and I wondered about the man in the next room who had ruined all my dreams, begged for help and forgiveness, knew my drink order better than I did, and knew by my eyes when I had a headache.

I thought back and remembered the countless gifts Mike had given to me that were perfect. I had never exchanged or returned any of them. I thought about the way he kept my car in perfect condition because I felt safer that way. I remembered him scratching the itchy spot on my back nearly every time we watched television. I remembered how he had made me grilled cheese sandwiches and crab legs every time I brought a baby home from the hospital. I remembered the cordless phone he had bought for me after I had my first baby, and the over-the-range microwave he surprised me with so that I could have more counter space. Almost every memory included Mike doing or saying something just perfect. Was it possible that he really did pay close attention to me? Could it be that he truly did love me? Could he mean it when he said I was important to him?

The fire was roaring by the time I finished my bath, so I sat on the thick rug next to Mike and stared at the flames as if mesmerized.

"Your eyes are like the blue part of a flame," I whispered. "I want to stare at them, but I am also scared because they burn."

"I don't want to scare you."

"I know. But the potential for joy is just as great as the potential for devastation. Just like a massive fire can be a great thing or a terrible thing. Fire burns away damaging weeds and stimulates germination, which brings healthy life to a prairie. But it also kills."

"I have something for you," Mike said reaching behind his back.

"You do?"

"Open it." He handed me a small package.

It was soft, and when I peeled off the wrapping a pair of pink socks fell into my lap. They were fuzzy and felt like a cloud brushing against my skin.

"I got lotion, too," he said, "so I can rub your feet. The socks have aloe in them, so you put them on after the foot rub, and I've been guaranteed that your feet will never feel the same."

"I love soft socks," I whispered, touched at the gift.

"I know." He laughed. "You have managed to fill two drawers with nothing but socks."

"I was hoping you wouldn't notice that." I smiled.

"Besides," he said, "I figured this would make the perfect gift. If you decide not to wear them, you could always throw them at me."

"Yeah, but I need a whole basket of them to make the right impact."

"Maybe you could just throw them over and over?"

"It might work. This time I'll get them dirty first, so I think I'll wear them right now."

"As you wish."

I still can't explain why I started crying. The tears came into my eyes, and I tried to blink them back, but it was useless. Before I knew it, my face and neck were soaked. Mike pulled me to him and stroked my hair.

"What's wrong?" he whispered.

"I hurt inside," I managed to say between sobs.

"I know it doesn't make it any better, but I will be sorry every day for the rest of my life to be the one to cause you this pain. Even though I hope for it, I know I have no right to ask for your forgiveness. All that stuff we talked about during the session today helps me understand what happened and why, but that doesn't make it go away. *Sorry* seems like such a small word, but I am sorry. So very, very sorry."

The tears flowed endlessly, and Mike silently cried with me.

The fire had dwindled to hot coals by the time I had cried myself out. My eyes were so swollen, I could barely see out of them, and I felt spent, like a flag after the wind stops. Mike carried me to the bed and gently tucked me in.

"Thank you for letting me hold you tonight," he whispered as he kissed my cheek. He tucked the covers tight against my back, the way I like them, and made himself comfortable on his mat on the floor. Sleep took me almost immediately, but, just before I lost contact with the world, I heard him say in a whisper so soft it might just as well have been a dream, "I will love you forever."

MIKE'S JOURNAL
3/25/2005

Sharla cried with me. The pain in her heart is so great. The sobbing, the emptiness—I will never forget one tear. It is the pain caused by my sin.

In my arms I held embodied hurt.

I am blessed to have a wife who will still share that intimacy of pain with me.

Lord, help me to never be on this side of the pain again.

MY STORY

"How can you even consider staying with him? What if he does something like this again?" It was not the first time I had been asked this question. Although we weren't close, I had known Jen for many years, and the question she raised was a good one. She had driven past my house on her way home from work and noticed me getting the mail out of the mailbox. She had pulled her car over for a quick chat, but we soon found ourselves in a deep conversation. I shivered and wrapped my jacket tightly around myself as I considered her question. Late March had surprised us with one last blizzard, and we had awoken that morning to seven inches of new, fluffy snow.

"Anybody might do something like this," I told her. "Even I might do something like this." While not a comforting thought, the marriage intensive we had recently returned from had taught me that every one of us is capable of great good as well as great damage. We are all just a few small choices away from causing destruction. Denying the potential we are capable of, good or bad, is where we get lazy.

The comment left my mouth before I fully realized how unsettling it would sound to Jen.

"There are people who don't do things like this," she responded. "My husband would never do this."

"Certainly. But anybody at any time *could* do something like this."
I could tell my comment shocked her, but I knew it was true. She
drove away fast and I knew that I had kicked her high horse. I stood
shivering in the snow struck by the truth I had just spoken as a jumble
of thoughts began to untwist themselves in my mind.

Mike had done wrong. Because of his hurtful and selfish choices,
my children and I had experienced great suffering. Could I be guaranteed that he would never hurt me again? Could I be guaranteed
that another man would be better?

Am I any better?

Just because I cannot, at this moment, comprehend my own de-
pravity does not mean that I am immune to it. Indeed, it is the very
act of denying the great evil I am capable of that makes me all the
more susceptible to its lure. The secret is not in ferreting out people
who are incapable of causing pain and surrounding myself with only
them, but in becoming a person who recognizes pain as the flip side
of joy. Like two sides of a coin, joy and pain are a package. I will experience both. If I am to tumble through life vulnerable to each injus-
tice, I will forever see myself as a helpless victim, unable to escape, let
alone choose my destiny. Rather, I need to forge myself into a complete person, whole within and, therefore, equipped to bear the evils
outside of myself. Only in this way can I ensure that I will survive, and
even thrive, during the darkness of life. I had excelled during the
joyful times. I was a kind, compassionate, and enjoyable person when
life was bright. But pain had begun to reveal my true character to me.

It was as if I was experiencing a prairie fire of my soul. The old
twisted weeds, my unhealthy thoughts and patterns, were being
burned away. I was staring at a field where I alone got to determine
what was allowed to germinate and grow. I told myself that if I was
smart I would use this chance to make sure what grew in me was
strong and healthy. I would use this opportunity to get rid of twisted,
sickly thoughts that snaked their way through my mind.

Mike had shown true repentance and remorse and an admira-
ble desire to work on his issues. Without being given any hope or

encouragement from me, he worked single-handedly on our marriage. He consumed counseling like a fire victim consumes fresh air. But, even with all of this, I could not be guaranteed that he would never hurt me in the future. That guarantee is not something that any person can make to another.

So, "What if he does this again?" is not the right question. The right question is: "Now, what is the right thing to do about what has happened?" I am not simply a victim in an out-of-control situation. I am not simply reacting. I get to make a decision out of the character of who I am and not out of the panic and hurt I am consumed by.

"What is the right thing to do about what has happened?" The question stood as tall as a mountain in my mind. While my body was frozen like a yard statue, my mind raced through endless options, none seeming to fit. Then I knew. "Do justly, love mercy, and walk humbly with my God." I was unsure of its exact location, but I knew it was a verse from the Bible, and the refrain filled my mind. "Do justly, love mercy, and walk humbly with my God." Although it wasn't a specific answer, there was no room for anything else in my mind.

Finally susceptible to the cold, I trudged through the snow and walked inside.

"Hey, Drake, what are you doing?" He was standing in a chair with soggy wrapping paper, tape, scissors, and a puddle of water spread across the table.

"I am wrapping Siah's birthday present."

I knew he was thinking about birthdays because everyone except me and Emery had recently celebrated a birthday, but I decided not to mention to Drake that he would need to wait eleven months to give his present to Josiah.

"What are you going to give him?"

"The snowballs," he told me as if the answer couldn't be more obvious.

"The snowballs?"

"Remember? The snowballs I made and put in the freezer."

"It worries me that that actually makes complete sense," I said as I soaked up the melted snowball. "I will be glad to have ice again, but we will have to figure out a solution to the wrapping problem later. We are going sledding at the Smileys."

The Smileys had been friends of ours since high school and owned a home out in the country with a perfect sledding hill in their backyard. When we arrived, their house smelled of cinnamon and pine, and the view out of their back windows was stunning. The untouched white snow glimmered and twinkled in the sunlight, and the frozen pond at the bottom of the hill begged to be skated on. It was a postcard kind of winter day with snowflakes on everyone's eyelashes, hot cocoa on the stove, and a warm fire blazing in the fireplace.

The kids couldn't get enough sledding, but one time of trudging back up the hill through thigh deep snow was enough for me. Our friends said they loved being outside in the snow, but I think they just wanted to give Mike and me some time alone by the fire. They are brilliant people, and their ulterior motives were sweet and kind.

After the feeling returned to my frozen fingers, I was able to move away from the fire to the large wall of windows and watch the kids as they laughed and tumbled in the snow. I felt Mike's warm hand on my back and, without thinking, leaned into his hug.

"They are great kids," he said, smiling out the window. "I don't deserve them."

"Nobody deserves kids like that," I agreed. "Mother Teresa wouldn't be worthy of them."

Makenna sailed down the hill with a shrill scream until her sled hit a divot in the snow and threw her off. Her sled continued straight toward the icy pond while she tumbled head over heels like a giant snowball, gaining momentum as she went. Just before she hit the hard ice, she miraculously came to a stop and quickly stood with her hands raised into the air as if she were a gymnast who had stuck the landing.

Laughing at her enthusiasm, Mike and I walked over to the fire to warm our feet. It was such a blustery day the cold seeped through the glass of the window and chilled us as we stood next to it.

"I want to thank you for not giving up on me yet," Mike said, warming my hand between his. "No matter what happens from this point forward, it means a lot to me that you have given me these last months."

"Yeah, they've been fun, haven't they?"

"Yeah," he laughed, "the kind of fun that could easily kill a person. It has been really hard for all of us, but for you it has been almost impossible. I'm astounded at your strength, your wisdom, and your grace. I want to look at you and say I'll never hurt you again, but I know I will. Not in the same way, but in some unintentional way, it will happen. You will hurt me, too.

"I've been thinking about our wedding day. When we said our vows, I thought I knew what we were promising each other, but I really had no idea. I basically stood up there in front of the preacher and God and promised that I would be perfect. I felt that I could be that for you. I gave you the impression that I could always put your needs above my own.

"I know now that I had no right promising such a thing. I can't promise you that I will always do the right thing, but I can promise that I will always try. I promise that I will do the hard work to completely understand why I did what I did and ensure that I rout it out of my life. I promise to apologize when I mess up, and I promise to stay around and fix the mess instead of leaving you to do it alone.

"And I promise to always love you with the kind of love that isn't fragile, but rugged and strong—the kind of love that grows stronger through difficult times and over the years. I can promise you a love that is complicated—not summed up by a simple word or statement, but a conglomeration of many thousands of looks, stories, words, touches, and memories that make up life. Our life."

His blue eyes burned as he whispered, "Whether you decide to remain my wife or not, I will love you forever."

As much as I wanted to reach out and comfort him, hardness waged a bitter war inside me. His sorrow and repentance were clear, and a deep change in his life had been evident over the last several months, but to grant forgiveness felt like giving away the only power that was mine.

I had seen a movie one time called *Amistad*, and there is a scene where the main character was in an impossible situation and he said that he would ask his ancestors for help. "They must come," he said, "for at this moment, I am the sole reason they ever existed at all." I thought about that. I thought about my mom and dad, grandparents, and great-grandparents, whose names I could not recall, and wondered what wisdom they would give to me if they were able. How would they wish for me to carry on their story? What would be my part in the legacy? What would I shout back in response to those who have gone before me?

And what would I pass on to my children, grandchildren and descendants? What will I say to them when they can no longer remember my name or hear my words? What will my story say?

I thought about the time I had crawled out onto the roof with Mike and eaten popcorn as we watched the sunset. I knew at that time that he was not safe. Ever since I was a teenage girl, I had admired him as you would a beautiful and wild wolf, for fear that his wild beauty had a dark side that was not to be tamed.

I thought about all the best stories, those in books, movies, or just stories of people I knew, and it struck me that life has a way of saying yes to the tame and no to the wild, but history says yes to the wild and forgets the tame completely.

This wild part of him was glorious and terrifying, mesmerizing and difficult. But it was the very thing that made him different from everybody else. Our story was a complicated one, and the future stood before me begging for a decision.

"I always used to feel as if I were a princess in a fairy tale," I told him. "You were my prince, and I was enchanted by you. That spell is broken. You are not a prince, I am not a princess, and this is no fairy tale. That sounds sad, but the true sad thing is living in a delusion, not knowing it, and believing that delusion to be true.

"To be honest, there are a lot of painful questions when a spell is broken, and I have been struggling with them for a long time now. I will probably never find the answers to my questions. What I know is that I'd rather have a real man than a fake prince."

In one fluid motion, Mike reached around my waist to pull me close and buried his face in my neck, his hot tears soaking my shirt. I hesitated for just a moment before putting both hands on his back and squeezing him to me.

"I didn't know if you would ever be ready for this," he said as he wiped his face on his sleeve. "I've been carrying it in my pocket every day for a couple of months now."

He reached into his pocket as he knelt to the floor. My breath caught when I saw a small silver circle in his outstretched hand. Without even meaning to, I reached for it and turned it to see the most gorgeous diamond ring I had ever seen.

"Will you take another chance on a future with me?" Mike whispered, scared to hear the answer. I slipped the ring on the finger that had been bare so long that the tan line had begun to disappear even through the dead of winter, and it fit perfectly. Surprised, since my fingers are small and I have always had a hard time fitting a ring, I raised my eyebrow in question as to how he had accomplished this. "I had it made for you. There isn't another ring like it anywhere in the world, and it should fit you perfectly."

I smiled. That seemed appropriate since our story was unlike any other but seemed to fit me.

"So, let's be real, and let's try again, Mike," I answered. "Let's write our future—not a fairy tale, but maybe a novel. Maybe even a classic."

PUZZLE

May is glorious in Iowa, and the smell of budding trees and new grass blew in the open windows. I had just poured the pieces to a beautiful horse puzzle onto the table when a group of college kids we had known for years burst into our living room.

"Hey, guys!" I smiled noting how tall they had grown. "You're just in time for a puzzle."

"Sweet," Frankie said, hugging all four kids at once. Frankie towered over everyone else in the room even though Mikey and JP seemed pretty tall to me. We had just started catching up on each other's lives when Emery suddenly stood straight up, much like a dog responding to a dog whistle, and said, "Oh! It's time to go scare the mailman!"

We all watched out the window and saw her run to the row of bushes by the side of the driveway and crouch down. She acted like this was a regular exercise, but none of us had witnessed it before. The mail truck slowly passed her and stopped by the mailbox just past our driveway. As the mailman focused on gathering envelopes with our address on them, Emery snuck quietly across the driveway and crouched just below the window in his door. He reached to open the mailbox, and Emery struck. She jumped up, screamed, and contorted her face into something monstrous.

From inside the house we heard the terrified shriek and watched mail fly around inside the truck. I was shocked that my sweet, quiet, youngest daughter had this operation on her usual activity list, but I couldn't help laughing along with everyone else in the room.

"That's the best thing I've seen since I've been home," Frankie said, as I tried to decide how angry the mailman might be and if it would affect my postal service.

"Well," Emery said as she walked back inside, cheeks rosy, "let's get back to that puzzle."

Four blond children squeezed in between the towering, muscular college boys at the table. I separated the straight pieces to the edge and handed them to Josiah, and I gave Emery the black pieces of the horse's body. I watched their hands open and receive the assorted puzzle pieces. A blue, sky piece snagged on my sleeve, and I looked at it. I took it to a chair by the window and tossed it back and forth in my hands. I stared at it – slightly fuzzy cardboard edges, thin paper pasted onto a brown back. I focused on the jig sawed holes as I realized my crucial mistake: I had given away pieces of myself.

Looking back I could clearly see that I had given pieces of myself to other people and expected them to handle those pieces with the care I demanded of them. I had given the responsibility of my happiness to my husband. An impossible job. And when he failed, I made him a prisoner of my anguish who would forever suffer my apathy. And, slowly, apathy crept into my soul and became my identity.

But I am the sole custodian of the pieces that constitute the puzzle of myself. I am the only one who can attend to my needs with the care that I demand. God has entrusted that job to me and to nobody else. And only by turning to Him to meet my needs am I fulfilled. My children are not responsible for my fulfillment. My husband is not responsible for my happiness.

I called to the pieces of myself that I had given away, and they returned. They made me whole and exposed the bitterness of the gray comfort I had established in myself. I was astonished at who I had settled into being.

MIKE'S JOURNAL
5/14/2005

I want to treat Sharla gently because I know I have crushed her deeply. I am scared of messing up. God, can you help me?

Sharla's needs are honesty, faithfulness, security, and protection. The simple things they include are: paying the bills on time, praying over the kids at night, being consistently kind and considerate, and telling her my struggles or temptations before they get out of control. I don't need to be perfect—just transparent.

I love her enough for this.

More than enough.

MOTHER'S DAY

"Hi, guys!" Mike called, walking ahead of me into the front door as we returned from the store. Looking around, he noticed the whole family except Josiah was together. "Josiah!" he called, "come here and we can all give Mom her cards!"

Hearing that, Emery burst into tears, grabbed Mike's hand, and dragged him up the steps and into her bedroom. Makenna, sobbing, grabbed my hand and dragged me back out the front door.

Josiah, oblivious to the drama, walked into the room everyone but Drake had just vacated. Through the screen door, I heard Drake tell Josiah, "I don't know how to explain what just happened in here."

"What is going on?" I asked Makenna.

"Well," she took a deep breath and then erupted. "The card Emery made you for Mother's Day got all wet. I saw it in the bathroom and took it to her. But she just started bawling when she saw it even though I told her I would help fix it. She yelled at me and said, 'I don't need your help! Just throw it away!' She was totally overreacting." Makenna took several deep breaths as tears spilled down her red cheeks before she continued. "I fixed all the flowers and words with my own markers and made it really pretty – even more pretty than Emery made it in the first place. But when I showed it to her she just bawled louder and ripped it into pieces! Even Drake tried to tell her that it looked nice, but Emery bawled and bawled. That's when Dad walked in and said it was time to give you your cards, and that's why Emery ran to her room. She ripped her card up so she doesn't have anything to give you. But Josiah didn't notice any of this stuff, so that's why he doesn't know what is going on. And Drake doesn't know how to explain it because he is a boy and doesn't even care that his card looks bad."

That night the kids and Mike cooked spaghetti and Emery frosted a cake in place of her card, and we laughed about the spectacle that had transpired earlier. The cards were sweet and cute. Even Drake's.

"You have one more gift," Mike told me. He placed a large box on the table in front of me, and I laughed at the wrapping made of old school assignments and duct tape.

"They are pictures of us, Mommy!" Emery sang.

"Quiet, Emery," Josiah said. "It's a surprise."

There were four large frames, each one with a black-and-white photo of one of the kids. The first one I picked up was a picture of Makenna lying on her belly on the floor with her head propped in her hands. Her fingerprints were stamped onto the left upper corner of the mat, and she had written, "I think my mom is a good mom and she is sweet," and signed her name in careful, pretty letters.

The picture of Josiah was a close-up of his face. His fingerprints were stamped along the right side of the mat.

"Josiah didn't want to do the writing, so he told me what to write and I did it for him," Mike told me. It said, "I get excited for Mom to sing her goodnight song," and Josiah had signed his name in all capital letters with a backward *J*.

Drake's picture was of him praying, and the fingerprints from both of his hands covered the bottom of the mat. Mike had written, "My Mommy is special to my heart," and Drake had signed his name with a tiny *D* and a very large *RAKE*.

In Emery's picture, she was standing in a tackle stance with a large smile. Her little handprints were stamped in the lower left corner and the upper right corner. Mike had written, "I tackle Mommy with hugs," and she had scribbled her name in tiny, deliberate scribbles.

"This is my favorite present ever," I said over the lump in my throat. "I love you guys so much. Mike, this was so thoughtful and had to take a lot of work. I love it. Thank you."

"Now let's eat cake," Drake said. And we did.

NEW PLAN

y parents had given us a gift card and generously offered to babysit while Mike and I enjoyed an evening out. We went to our favorite Mexican restaurant and agreed to use the time talking about anything except our marriage problems.

"Your chin looks terrible," Mike said after we were seated in our booth. "It has to hurt."

"Yeah, it does," I agreed, gently sucking Dr. Pepper through a straw. I had splashed hot oil on my face the night before attempting to learn to cook fish – a dish I had never mastered. My lips were swollen and blistered, and my entire chin and neck were covered with bright, angry blisters that not only looked, but also felt, extremely painful.

"What?" I asked Mike when I noticed he was looking at me with an odd expression on his face.

"Um, what are you doing?"

"It feels good," I explained as I rolled the cup full of icy soda lightly against the burned areas on my chin and neck.

"Well, it is going to be hard to take you seriously while you're doing that, but there is something we need to talk about," Mike said, dipping a chip into the spicy salsa.

"Okay," I said returning the cup to the table. "What's wrong?"

"We can't continue like this," Mike stated bluntly after a deep breath. "My paycheck from the lumberyard isn't enough. You can't work because we can't afford the childcare. We already gave up all of our insurance, which I don't feel good about. I just don't know how we are going to make it."

"I know. I hate it that we are in debt like we are." We had made it a personal goal to never aquire debt, and until we had to hire a lawyer, we had achieved that goal. However, debt is a slippery slope. We had sold everything we could think of selling and had trimmed back our monthly budget to a painful degree. We lived frugally, only turning on lights when absolutely necessary and using the heater or air conditioner so sparingly the temperature threatened to affect our health. Still, it was not enough. I had used our credit card to pay for a doctor's appointment, and for the first time, we could not pay the bill when it arrived in the mail. Then I had to use the credit card to buy new shoes for Josiah, who had grown two sizes in four months. And Makenna needed bigger jeans. The needs just kept coming.

"Even if I request extra hours, it won't make enough of a difference," Mike said, rubbing his hand through his hair.

"Maybe we should sell our house," I desperately suggested.

"Our payment is so small right now that it would cost us more to live in an apartment. We bought our house right."

"Remember, though, when we sold our house in Omaha we made money. With all the renovations we've done, we could probably make a profit and pay off our debt." I racked my mind trying to come up with other solutions that didn't seem so drastic, but nothing came to me. I heard the sizzling of the fajitas headed to our table and moved the basket of chips to the side.

"I guess it is worth thinking about," Mike grudgingly admitted, "but then we would have to figure out somewhere to live. It would be hard to beat what we are currently paying."

"I have an idea!" I felt excited at my sudden inspiration and reached for the salsa to drench my fajita. "You're friends with a lot of really successful businessmen. Why don't you meet with some of those guys, like Pete, Jeff, and Simon, and ask them what they would do if they had to start all over. They're obviously smart, and they know what is working right now, so their advice could be very helpful." I loved my food spicy, but had to down half of my drink to quench the fire in my mouth.

"That's a really good idea." Mike smiled, but we had no idea at the time that following this course of action would change everything.

MIKE'S JOURNAL
5/29/2005

If a thought is rooted mainly in feelings, it is probably a lie. If I think I am unimportant to Sharla and the only thing I have to support that thought is a feeling instead of an honest conversation or another factual event, then I need to recognize that the feeling I am experiencing is a lie and will only lead me to destruction and cause me to do damage. I am responsible for the feelings I have, and I need to sift through which ones to keep and which to get rid of.

I have found that it is not easy to get rid of feelings even when I recognize that they are most likely untrue. My temptation is to take them to Sharla and make her accountable for them or want her to fix them. Instead, what I have been learning to do is to find a logical avenue out of the feeling—some kind of handhold that is bigger than my feeling. When I feel unimportant to her, I remind myself of all the times she stuck by me, all the times she went out of her way to invest in us, or even the things she is probably doing right now at home that barely register to me most of the time.

These facts keep the thoughts free from feelings that lie.

NEW LIFE

"Nobody move!" I said to the kids who were scattered around the kitchen. "There's a wasp."

"I'll get it Mom," Drake said, wielding a pair of scissors.

"No, it might sting you. Just hand me the flyswatter please," I instructed.

"I can cut it," he said.

"Drake, no. Don't irritate it."

"I got it!" Drake announced.

"What?" I asked, astounded. "Did you really just cut a wasp in half while it was flying?"

"Yep."

I bent to my knees and spotted two halves of a wasp lying on the linolium floor.

"How did you do that," I asked, astonished.

"I'm a ninja," Drake said. "I've done that one time before. And now I'll never do it again so my record will be one hundred percent."

"Oh no!" Makenna shouted from her tiptoes atop a chair she had scooted to the pantry. I looked just in time to see the box of cornstarch fall from the top shelf and explode across the floor.

"Oh, Makenna!" I helped her off the chair and grabbed a broom. "Watch this!" I swept the cornstarch into a pile in the center of the kitchen, grabbed a cup of water and a spoon. Sitting next to Makenna, I began to slowly spoon drops of water onto the white, fluffy powder.

"What are you doing?" Makenna asked.

"Mix that together with your hands." As her small fingers mixed the concoction, a slimy paste began to form.

"It behaves like a solid and a liquid," I told her. "You can touch it and mold it like a solid, but, when you stop molding it, it flows like a liquid. Almost like it melts."

"Weird!" Makenna laughed, watching the ball she had formed seemingly melt and drip through her fingers.

"It's not a true mixture; it is a suspension. That's why it reacts so uniquely."

"It's fun," Makenna said, ignoring my attempt to educate her and letting the goo drip down her arm to her elbow.

When the phone rang, I quickly washed my hands and told Makenna to let the other kids play with the goo too.

"You'll never believe what just happened!" Mike said when I finally answered the phone.

"Is it good or bad?" I asked, holding the phone between my ear and shoulder as I pointed the kids to the kitchen floor.

"It's unbelievable."

"That doesn't answer the question," I said.

"Just listen. I'm in the Roosevelt area on my bike, and I can't wait till I get home to tell you this."

"You rode your bike from work all the way to the Roosevelt area?"

"Yeah. But that's not what I want to tell you."

"Okay, that is crazy, but go ahead with your story."

"You know how we decided that I should meet with some of the guys I know who would be able to give me some good business advice? Well, I had a meeting with Simon after work today, which is why I rode my bike down here. Anyway, I asked him what advice he could give me, and he asked me what I would do in the business world if I could do anything. I told him that I had no idea and the only thing you and I have talked about was selling our house because we could make a nice profit with all the improvements we've made.

"We talked for a long time and he asked a lot of questions. Then, he told me that he had read my story in the newspaper. We've known each other since high school, so when he saw my name, it caught his attention. He felt in his heart that my story was not over. He told God that if there was something he could do to be a part of my restoration, he would be honored.

"Then he told me that he wants to buy a house for us to fix up. He will use his money to buy it and pay for the improvements, and when we sell it, we can pay him back and keep the profit. He will do that for five houses, and by then we should be able to start a small business and run it on our own."

Mike and I walked in a daze for the next few days and wondered if we had misunderstood the conversation. We couldn't think of any reason that somebody as successful as Simon would be so generous to us. Most of the people we had known avoided us, so it was a shock to be treated with respect and generosity. We talked it over until we convinced ourselves that Simon hadn't meant what he had said. We decided that he had probably gotten caught up in the moment and regretted his impulsiveness when he thought about it later. Then Mike answered his phone.

"Hey, it's Simon."

"Hi. What's up?"

"I have your first house."

"What?" Mike mouthed too quietly to be heard.

"Are you there?" Simon asked. "I said I have your first house."

"What do you mean?" Mike finally managed to respond.

"I mean that I found a house that would be great for what we were talking about, and I talked to the owner. We agreed on a great price, so you just need to go look at it and tell me if you want it. I am ready to sign the papers tonight if you give me the go-ahead."

The house turned out to be a lovely run-down home in a beautiful area of town. Thus began our new life.

TRIPLE BRAIDED CORD

On a sweaty, hot day in September, almost a year after our crisis began, we had a sweet ceremony in a park to renew our vows. We weren't done working through all the issues, but we had decided that our marriage was worth the effort it would take to make it work. The ceremony was not a statement that everything was better, but a statement that our vows were once again in effect. We sent no invitations, yet dozens of our family and friends showed up and supported us. It was humbling and special. Makenna and Emery stood up with me on my side, and Drake and Josiah stood on Mike's side. We didn't promise to be perfect. We didn't promise to always put the other's needs above our own. We promised to honor God and each other, and we promised to apologize after our failures. We promised to let love win.

The triple-braided cord had not broken; it had saved us.

MAILING A LETTER

I convinced my sore muscles to rally one more time and climbed into the beat-up, oversized pickup Mike had purchased after we sold our first house. Simon, good to his word, had helped us with buying five houses. It took us a year and a half, and, after that, we were able to operate a small business on our own. The work was demanding, and the learning curve was steep. We spent our days sanding, scraping, painting, cleaning, sawing, nailing, and building. We toned muscles we didn't remember having and woke up each morning stiff and sore.

Due to exhaustion, we didn't have a lot of time to work through the consequences of our marriage crisis. The decision to stay together was made, but I often struggled with my feelings toward Mike. I had decided to forgive him, but I didn't know how to love him again. When I thought of him, I felt nothing. I went through the motions, and I trusted God to restore our marriage, but I continued to feel empty and alone.

After a particularly stressful day of attempting to rid an attic of a family of raccoons, Mike and I were taking a quick trip to the grocery store near our house to mail a letter. It had been a week of punishing work and long hours. I knew I was overreacting, but I had gotten my feelings hurt by some of Mike's joking earlier in the day, so I decided to talk to Mike about it.

"You've been pretty sarcastic today," I said as I fastened my seat-belt and grimaced in pain at the movement. I had painted ceilings the day before and, consequently, my shoulders fiercely resisted motion of all sorts.

"Have I hurt your feelings?" he asked, surprised.

"Yeah. I know you were just joking, but it just doesn't feel funny anymore."

"Wow. I am really sorry. I had no idea." He pulled up in front of the grocery store and put the truck in park.

"I know. I usually don't get upset about this sort of thing, but it has just been a long day. Do you think you can just stop making sarcastic comments for the rest of today?"

"Absolutely. I'm really sorry that I hurt you, and I will only say nice things for the rest of today. You don't need to worry about a thing."

I smiled at him and opened the passenger door so I could slide out and quickly slip the letter into the mailbox. However, as I slid down the vinyl, my shorts got caught on the lever that controls the seat. Since I am a short person, my feet did not touch the ground, and I was dangling from the seat lever by my shorts. I tried to wiggle and release my shorts, but that caused the lever to slide deeper into my shorts.

I considered all my options in a split second and decided to try wrenching my body back and forth angrily. Instead of solving my problem and gently releasing my shorts, this decision caused the seat, and my body with it, to lurch back and forth as if possessed.

As I dangled, with one side of my shorts hiked up to my hip-bone, being tossed violently back and forth, the irony struck me. I thought about the conversation I had just had with Mike and thought about what he must be seeing at the moment. I thought about his promise to only say nice things the rest of the day, and I began to laugh.

At that moment my shorts ripped, and I was dropped unceremoniously to the concrete. I was laughing hard. I hit the ground hard. I had given birth to four children. It happened. I wet my pants.

I was terrifyingly aware that this event was unfolding just a few steps from the front door of my regular grocery store—the store where the employees knew me by name.

I was laughing too hard to say anything, but I managed to worm my way back into the truck, letter still in hand, and motioned for Mike to drive away.

"Sometimes the things you ask of me are impossible," Mike said as he bit his lips together and drove away.

FLAT

"I noticed you haven't worn the new shirt I got you. Doesn't it fit?" I asked Mike as we got into the car. Each of the kids had been invited to do something with friends, so we decided to go for a drive. Some of our best conversations took place in a car. If we stayed home, household projects became a distraction.

"Oh." Mike sighed looking over his shoulder to back the car out of the driveway. "It fits."

"If you don't like it, I can return it."

"No." Mike breathed a deep breath and then blew it out all at once. "It's orange."

"I know," I smiled. "I love orange. It's my favorite color."

"I thought your favorite color was yellow."

"Well, actually I keep alternating between yellow and red, but recently I began thinking about how orange is a combination of both so I decided that would be my new favorite color."

"Ironic."

"You don't like orange?"

"I always used to. But I haven't worn orange for years."

"Seriously?" I asked, turning my gaze from out the window to look at Mike. "Why ... oh. Did you wear orange when you were in jail?"

"Yeah."

"They literally put orange on you? I thought that was just on TV."

"Nope. Everyone gets an orange jumpsuit. You probably didn't notice, but I threw out every piece of clothing I had that was orange after that. I didn't actually have that many things, only a couple T-shirts. But I haven't worn that color since that day."

"I'm sorry. I never stopped to think about that. I can return the shirt."

"Don't. It's time to move on. I need to cross this bridge. It's silly to eliminate a color from my wardrobe just because it brings back bad memories. Besides," he said, grabbing my hand, "it's my wife's favorite color."

"Okay. But if you change your mind, I can easily return it."

"I won't." Mike smiled at me. "So, how is it going?"

"Fine."

"I mean how is it going with us? How do you feel we are doing together? As a couple?"

"Oh." I hesitated wondering how honest to be. "You know I have a personal reluctance to visit those darker emotions."

"Oh, yes." Mike laughed. "I do know that about you. But you still need to answer the question."

"Well, I think we live together really great. I feel like I have forgiven you, and I don't think I'm holding on to any bitter feelings."

"But?" Mike asked quietly, raising one eyebrow.

"But," I continued slowly, "it feels flat. I'm sorry. I wish it didn't. It just feels hollow. It's been five years, and I keep expecting my feelings to catch up with my decisions, but nothing happens."

"Have I been doing anything wrong?" Mike asked, clearly pained.

"No, nothing. In fact, you've been doing everything right. You've been supportive, helpful, encouraging, engaged. In fact," I admitted after rolling it over in my head, "I really prefer this new you to the man I was married to before the crisis. I think all the counseling we went through changed some things that I didn't even know we needed to change. If I could choose between the you of before and the you of now, I would chose this guy."

"What do you think has changed?"

"Hmm." I mulled it over. "You seem to be more at peace with who you are. I think in the past you felt like you had to prove yourself. Now you just are."

He laughed. "There's really no use trying to prove yourself when you blow it so big that everyone you know is completely aware of how messed up you are. At that point you can only accept that you will never be able to be what everybody expects of you, and you just feel thankful for those people who stick with you."

"Well, I like that better. It's less stressful." I smiled at him.

"Do you want to drive through Friedrichs?" Mike asked, gesturing toward our favorite coffee shop.

"Yes! We are probably the only people in America who go to coffee shops but don't like coffee."

"I know, but they have great chai." He drove the car around the coffee shop and, by memory, ordered my favorite hot tea drink.

"So," he asked handing me my drink, "you still feel like it's flat even though you prefer now to then?"

"I know it sounds confusing," I admitted, blowing on my hot drink. "I really think that if we could have gotten to where we are another way, I would be exceedingly happy. But it feels like something deep inside of me is broken. Sort of like I have lost the ability to be in love. I can appreciate you, be proud of you, have a good time with you, even depend on you, but I just can't be in love with you. The love I used to have for you felt powerful and consuming. Now, although I think a lot of good things about you, the fire is gone. I'm full of ashes. I wish it wasn't true, but it is. Does that hurt you?"

"It makes me sad because I feel the complete opposite. I am so in love with you I can hardly think straight. You are everything to me. You are all that matters and all that I think about. I love you so much more now than I ever have before. I am horrified that I have broken some part of you. It makes me angry at myself and sad for you." He grabbed my hand as he pulled the car onto a small gravel road and stopped. "I understand it though. I understand why you would feel flat and broken. I am so sorry. Do you want out of this?"

"No. I haven't come this far to quit now. I figure that everything will eventually fall into place if I just keep making healthy decisions for myself. I read a book called *The Prophet* recently, and in it the author said, 'God will fill you with love, but that does not always mean you will feel love.' I think that is true. If I have faith that I will feel in love with you again, then maybe someday I will. If not, it is still love. It's just a love that feels different."

"That would be excellent for me, and I am more than happy to take whatever you feel that you can give me without pushing for more. But that sounds terrible for you. I don't want the rest of your life to be flat."

"But the thing is, I like who you are now. I don't want to end up with anybody else because everybody has issues. If I married someone else, I am sure that person would come with baggage. At least I know your issues, and I know you are willing to work them out. It might be different if I felt that you hadn't changed or weren't willing to work on yourself. It might even be different if I felt that who you had become was someone I didn't like, but I do. I just need to get over how we got here. That is where I am stuck."

"I will do anything. I will go to counseling, conferences, read books, anything you feel would help."

"I know."

"I thank God for you every single day. I'm still shocked at the poise and grace you have. Every once in a while I run into someone I used to go to group therapy with, and every time I've been shocked at how much better my life has gotten since the last time I saw any of them."

"What ever happened to that guy that started at the same time you did? I think his name was Rob."

"Yeah, Rob. I'm really worried about him actually. The last time I called him the number had been disconnected. Nobody has heard from him."

"Do you think he might do something stupid?"

"That's what concerns me. Maybe I should go drive around where he last lived. Maybe someone knows something."

"That's a good idea. I know some of those guys should never be trusted, but they aren't all like that. I feel bad that people just stamp the label of sex offender on them and then treat them as if they are horrible humans. Someone needs to help guys like Rob."

"I'll go tomorrow."

MIKE'S JOURNAL
4/20/2009

I hadn't heard from Rob for over a year, so I went out to the last place I knew he was living. It's a good thing I did. When I got there, I found him in an old barn. He's been sleeping on a cot and using the fireplace I gave him a long time ago for heat. He hadn't talked to a human in over four months.

He told me that he had decided nobody cared about him so he should either live like he wanted to or die. His plan was to flip a coin at sunset. Heads meant suicide. Tails meant driving into town and giving in to the temptations that have been plaguing his mind. By tomorrow he would have been dead or in jail. And an innocent person may have been damaged.

When I walked in the door, he broke down crying. Nobody else has visited him. I was able to talk him out of it, but I can't be there for him like he needs.

There's no reason that couldn't have been me.

GRANDMA

"**I**s Grandma still sick?" Emery asked as she climbed into the van.

"She isn't really sick, honey," I explained as I buckled her seatbelt. "She is just old."

"She must be as old as you can get," she said, her fine blond hair blowing in the wind.

The drive to Grandma's made me nostalgic. I had hundreds of memories of Grandma making pie, canning vegetables, sewing, and hanging laundry on the line in the backyard. Now she was unable to leave her chair, and she usually fell asleep during our visits.

"Oh, look," I told Emery as I drove into the driveway, "Uncle Michael is here, too."

We walked around to the back door, as always, and found my brother Michael and Grandpa carrying a load of freshly picked tomatoes into the house.

"You're just in time," Michael said as he placed a bunch of tomatoes into my arms. "Grandpa is a machine."

"He takes his garden seriously," I agreed, grabbing a tomato that threatened to fall.

"Sharla, you're going to need to take some of these tomatoes with you when you go," Grandpa told me as we unloaded our burden onto the kitchen counter.

"Sure thing." As long as I have lived, I have never tasted tomatoes equal to Grandpa's.

"Say, Sharla," Grandpa asked as he loaded tomatoes into a paper sack, "do you still shop at that grocery store down the street from you?"

"Yes, quite often. I recently had an unfortunate incident there while trying to mail a letter."

"There is a cashier who works there named Dorothy. She was in my Sunday school class for, oh, probably twenty years or more. I heard she was sick. Have you seen her recently?"

"Um, she is … " I hesitated. The familiar nervousness permeated my muscles, and my mind turned to metal. A flashback popped into my mind of practicing the delivery of bad news with Makenna and the stuffed bear, Bruce, and I decided to try Makenna's method. "If you want to see her again, you'll have to do it in heaven."

"What?" Grandpa and Michael asked in unison.

"Well … she … you see," I stammered. "The situation is not positive."

"Did she die?" Michael asked.

I nodded. "That is it exactly."

"Why didn't you just say she died?" Grandpa asked.

"Oh, I know better. Saying that will get you into trouble."

"What are you talking about?" Michael asked, confused.

"One time a friend of mine died so I told Mom that she was dead, and Mom started bawling and said I needed to ease into news like that."

"Ha!" Grandma laughed from the other room. Even though I knew what to expect, I was shocked at the paper-thin skin draped over her bones. Her cheeks were sunken and pale, but her glassy, blue eyes lit up when she saw us.

"Why, hello, Sharla," she said so quietly I had to bend near her to hear. "And who do we have here? Is that Emery?"

"Hi, Grandma. Can I play with your marbles?"

"The kids love the marbles." Grandma laughed. "Of course you can, honey. You know where to find them. Sharla, you sound just like your grandpa," Grandma said as I sat next to her. "He was taking care of Uncle Dan's dog while their family was on vacation one time. But the dog suddenly died. I told him he needed to be careful how he broke the news when Dan called. So that night, I heard Grandpa tell Dan that the dog had *absconded*. Well, that was terrible. They didn't understand what he was trying to tell them, and the whole thing turned into a big mess."

"I can relate to that," I said.

"I'll start making the popcorn," Grandpa announced, although it was only ten in the morning.

"He loves any excuse to make popcorn," Grandma said.

"How are you doing, Grandma?" I asked.

"I had a small cold last week, but I am fine now." She smiled.

"You are like a tennis ball, Grandma. You always bounce back," Michael told her.

"More like a bowling ball." Grandma chuckled.

I pulled my chair closer, so I could hear her soft voice better.

"Sharla, I want to tell you something about being married: it's hard. I love your Grandpa, and I always have. But he is a hard man to live with. We all have troubles. The answer is not in another person. It is in yourself."

"I know, Grandma," I said as I smoothed her transparent skin across the back of her hand. "But it seems impossible sometimes. I've decided to make it work between us, but sometimes it gets overwhelming and hard. I'm stuck. I didn't want it to be like this. I didn't want this to be our story."

"Well," she said, pinning me with her bright, clear eyes, "We fall in love in an instant, and then spend the rest of our lives working to stay that way."

"You don't waste words." I laughed at her bluntness.

"I don't have enough energy to waste words. I just have to say what I have to say." I smiled at her as she nodded off into a deep sleep.

"Looks like I will be eating your popcorn," I whispered to her.

ARMPIT HAIR

If forgiveness were easy it wouldn't be worth very much. It wouldn't require us to put our selfishness away and suffer growing pains as we mature. It certainly wouldn't have sent an innocent man to die on a cross. As it is, forgiveness is pretty much priceless.

I thought about what Grandma had told me: "We fall in love in an instant, and then spend the rest of our lives working to stay that way." Was I unsatisfied with my current feelings because I was comparing them to that instant I fell in love? Was I wasting my energy wishing for a different story instead of working with the one I had? Probably.

"Mom!" Emery called from her bedroom, "I'm ready for bed."

My deep thoughts scattered as I climbed the steps to the kids' rooms and heard the boys arguing with each other.

"What is going on in here?" I asked, stepping inside the doorway.

"Drake wants the door open, but I want it shut because I can't fall asleep with all the light from the hallway," Josiah explained, clearly frustrated.

"But I don't like the room that dark," Drake complained. "With the door shut it is so dark I can't even see my hand in front of my face. It is freaky."

I sighed. "Well, you both have a good point. I can't choose between those two options, so you guys will have to work this out, but you need to do so in a calm and open-minded manner. I am going to go tuck Emery in, and I will check back after I am done to see what you decided, but if I hear you arguing and being mean to each other I will make each of you pluck out an armpit hair. Consider this a warning."

"What?" Drake yelled. "I only have one and it just grew in this week! I can't pull him out! I can't be armpit bald!"

"Then you need to work this out reasonably."

I wondered about the sanity of what I had just said as I walked into Makenna's room.

"How is it going, Angel Face?"

"Math teachers are *so* the opposite of me. I don't understand this, and I have twenty-seven problems left. I have to write out each step, and I hate it."

I tried not to groan as flashbacks of my own struggles with math assaulted me. "That just buzzes your button, doesn't it?"

"What?"

"Isn't that an expression?"

"Um, no."

"Well, I'm sure you'll figure it all out." I tried to sound certain, knowing full well I had never conquered math. "I will give you another half hour, but then you should go to sleep."

"Fine." She rolled her eyes and looked back down at her math book.

"All right, Emery," I said stepping into her tidy room. "I'll bet you are really tired."

"Actually, I am uptight," she answered with a sigh.

"Uptight?" I tried not to laugh. "What's wrong?"

"We have to run a mile in PE tomorrow. I don't think I can do it. You know how I hate running and how clumsy I am. What if I fall down? Or what if I can't finish?" She threw herself onto her bed and I spread the covers over her, tucking them in tightly around her shoulders.

"I am sure you will do just fine. I've seen you run, and I think you are pretty fast. Besides, you can do anything you put your mind to."

"Maybe," she said. "But I can't do plumbing."

I laughed. "No, but nobody really expects you to do any plumbing."

"Okay." She rubbed her eyes, and said her prayers. I gave her the good-night kiss, which was three short kisses on the cheek, then a butterfly kiss, followed by one long kiss on the cheek, and I made a display out of looking under her bed and in her closet, as usual, before I turned off her light.

I went back to check on the boys and noticed Mike had come home and was saying their prayers with them.

"What did you decide to do about the door?" I asked when they were done.

"Dad," Josiah explained, "we were fighting over the door because I wanted it shut and Drake wanted it open. Then Mom told us to figure it out without fighting. She said if we fought about it, she would make us each pull out an armpit hair. So we talked about it reasonably and decided to shut it part way."

"We discussed it reasonably and with open minds so we get to keep our armpit hair," Drake confirmed.

Mike tried valiantly to keep from laughing, but was forced to turn and face the wall with his hand over his mouth. His shoulders shook, and I had to bite the inside of my cheeks until I could speak seriously.

"You guys did great, and I am proud of you," I told them.

"Yeah," Mike echoed, still facing the wall. "We are seriously proud parents."

"And I am glad, too," announced Drake, "because I just got my first armpit hair, and I named him yesterday."

"You named your armpit hair?" I asked.

"Yeah. His name is Norman." Drake rubbed his eyes and snuggled into his blankets.

"Well, you and Norman need to get to sleep, so good night. I love you guys."

"Night, Mom." The boys yawned in unison.

"Armpit hair?" Mike asked as we walked down the steps toward the kitchen.

"I don't know what happened. It just came to me," I explained as I grabbed the popcorn and stuck it in the microwave.

"Well, it worked. I can never predict the things you do around here."

I looked at Mike as he poured us both a drink and took them to the TV, and I wondered if I still felt flat about him. There were moments, like tonight, when we were doing life together—just trying our best to make it. Moments when we knew each other so well we didn't have to ask, "What do you want to drink?" or, "What show do you want to watch?" because years of life had already taught us the answer. In those moments I was tempted to feel close to him and alive with him. But, before the feeling could really happen, I shot it down in a panic. Reluctant to fall from such a height, I kept my feelings from soaring too high. I pushed the thought to the back of my mind and carried the popcorn to the TV and snuggled on the couch looking forward to *M*A*S*H* reruns.

DIG

"You'll never believe what just happened," Mike said, closing the front door against the humid Iowa summer. "I'll give you a hint. It involves Cliff."

"Oh, did his air conditioning go out again? I thought you fixed that a couple of days ago." I finished cutting a watermelon into slices and placed them on a plastic tray to carry to the kids in the backyard. Makenna was trying to get a tan by the pool, but the boys weren't letting their thirteen and fourteen years of maturity stop them from making a huge mud puddle in the middle of what had the potential to be a garden. Emery chose the mud puddle over the tan, and all three looked like sweaty mud monsters.

"I saw Cliff walking toward me when I drove in, and he was standing by my truck before I could even get out. I expected him to tell me about some new problem he has, but he didn't. He told me that he just wanted me to know I was one of the best friends he has ever had, and I was one of the best surprises of his later life. He said he never expected to make a new friend being the age he is, and he never expected it to be someone so much younger. He laughed about that day when he told me I was a bad man and said he couldn't have been more wrong."

"Really? Cliff said that?"

"Yeah. He said I am a good man and he considers himself lucky to count me as one of his friends."

"Wow. That had to be nice to hear."

"It was nice. I certainly wouldn't call myself a good man, but it was nice of him to say that."

"That's it!" I yelled. "I get it now."

"What?" Mike asked, eyebrows scrunched.

"Stay here. Don't move."

I ran to my bedroom and opened my closet. I looked on the top shelf behind a stack of folded sweatshirts and found what I was looking for. I grabbed the small book and ran back to Mike.

"Look." I waved the book at him.

"What is it?"

"My journal. I filled it up a long time ago and haven't looked at it in years. But I just thought of something." I flipped through the pages until I found what I was looking for. "This entry is from the night you confessed to me. It's long, but basically I went through all the good things in my life and said good-bye to all of them. Here, read this part at the end."

"Are you sure you want me to read your journal?" Mike asked.

"Yes." I shoved the book at him. "Read this part at the bottom of the page after I've said good-bye to all the good things in my life."

"I am going to bury you, and the grave will hold you tight," Mike read aloud. "You won't be alone—the best part of me will be with you."

"See?" I asked.

"No," Mike said. "What is important about this right now?"

"When you were talking about Cliff calling you a good man, it made me remember that I buried all the good feelings in my life. And I buried the best part of me. That's why I've felt flat. That's why I feel gray and dull. I'm buried. I have to dig myself up."

THE WORK OF PAIN

I am often tempted to live my life divided between the easy emotions of anger or joy. I sometimes want to be mad, and I sometimes want to be happy. I never want to be both at the same time, but I often find that I am. My path has been crooked and unpredictable. Life never follows a straight road, and I have rarely ended up where I expected to. I think God used my convoluted path as a tool to scrape off my hard edges and teach me the less straightforward skills like patience, forgiveness, understanding, and perspective.

I felt flat because I had said good-bye to joy and insulated myself from the pain I wanted to deny. It was as if pain and I had become unwilling roommates – I knew I lived with pain, but I was loath to look it in the eye. I shunned it and hoped my indifference would make it go away. Pain is a stubborn roommate though and, instead of vanishing, it persistently intruded, thrusting my happiness down. I resented the space it occupied in my story. But joy and pain cannot be selectively chosen: they are flip sides of each other. If you open your door to joy, pain will enter as well.

When the earth grows colder and the days grow shorter, the trees experience a reduction in the saturation level of chlorophyll and are forced to let the green color seep from their leaves. The foliage grows colorful and glorious, and, although the shortened daylight will eventually wither their leaves, the trees will not throw themselves to the ground and die. They will bear the season and continue to shout their story of life.

The chemical compound copper sulfate is a rich, blue color, but it is also toxic. Nature often combines the good with the bad like this. It is as if the very earth is screaming to us to look more closely and deeply. Nothing is as it first appears. "Don't miss the wondrous just because it is complex," the earth shouts. It is more often than not the difficult path that brings to light the brilliance of life.

Love came to me dressed as passion and adventure, but then it ravaged my heart and my soul, burning fiercely until, in shock, I looked around and discovered myself in a wasteland of ash. Then I shunned the hollowness left by pain and filled what was left of my heart with dull, gray ashes to keep it safe. It felt easy. I cursed the ashes, hated the ashes, and then clung to them so that I would not disappear. I inhaled them and fused to them until my apathy became a comfortable companion.

No more.

I finally allowed pain to have its way. I didn't separate myself from it, but, instead, I sanctioned it to do its work. I accepted the anguish of it into my story. Against every defensive instinct, I allowed pain to scrape and chisel at the core of who I was. It nearly killed me.

Copper sulfate reacts when it encounters an outside agent. When exposed to a flame, the blue color turns white. When exposed to hydrochloric acid, it turns green. When exposed to magnesium or aluminum, it forms copper. When I was exposed to pain, my nature had reacted strongly and violently, but the result was something better. I was deeper, richer, and wiser. I understood more about myself, others, nature, God, and life. I believed I had bequeathed a generous gift of forgiveness to my husband, but when I looked closer and with more understanding, I realized that I was an echo in a bigger story of forgiveness. I was a character in a story that was as old as the world.

I let go of the things I thought I needed to feel happy. I wiped away my expectations and my desires. I released Mike from the responsibility of keeping me happy. I released my kids, friends, and family from that responsibility, too. I released the fantasy of what I wished I had. I focused on the true source of happiness. I felt the tether tighten, and, like a kite, I soared.

THE PICTURE

When I look back on the day of my wedding, I am astounded at how much I did not know. When I said, "I do," I thought the most stressful part of being married would be planning the wedding.

My marriage has brought me romantic trips to exciting places. Long bike rides. Deep conversations. Teamwork. Someone to take care of me when I am sick or tired. Laughter. A soul mate. A different perspective. A full heart. A true companion.

It also brought me arguments that made me want to spit. Differences of opinion that seemed insurmountable. Agony that ripped the breath from me.

There have been times I was certain beyond any doubt that our marriage was over. There have been times I wished our marriage was over. But, always, there was just a little something to fight for. Sometimes that little something was no more than a small hope of friendship. Sometimes it was pure desperation and the stubborn hatred of giving up. Sometimes it was four small faces. And as we struggled and toiled, that small little something would grow.

Looking back at the path we traveled together, a picture is apparent. Some of our path is washed with bright, cheerful colors. Other parts are filled in with rich, vibrant hues. I experienced the darkest of black and wallowed in the gray of ash.

But when I step back and look at the picture we have made, the only thing I notice is an old brown cross.

The brilliance is almost blinding.

A NOTE FROM THE AUTHOR

This story is written from my point of view. I was able to rely on journals I kept as well as the ones Mike kept to portray thoughts and feelings accurately. I was able to rely on documentation I saved from the state appointed counselor to accurately portray the legal process as well as the sex offender program. For the stories involving the kids, I was able to rely on a book I've constantly kept in which I wrote the amusing things they said or did.

I have changed some of the names for the sake of privacy.

To help the story flow, I combined some events. For instance, the bed and breakfast we stayed at during the intensive did not have a fireplace. The scene in front of the fireplace happened at my parents' house the night we returned from the intensive. Also, although most of the anonymous Christmas presents for the kids were dropped off on Christmas Eve, some were delivered days earlier. I tried to keep the minor inaccuracies small and insignificant.

Thank you for reading my book. I appreciate the gift of your time.